Inside the Wall

A Memoir

By

Megan Bishop-Scott

Original cover art

by John Warner Scott 1991

ISBN-13: 978-0-9879600-1-6

This book is dedicated to

Paramahamsa Nithyananda

And the Lineage of Enlightened Masters

Who have protected and guided me

On this amazing journey

"Come to the edge," he said.

They said, "We are afraid."

"Come to the edge", he said.

They came, he pushed them, and they flew".

~Apollinaire, Guillaume

(1880 – 1918)

PART ONE:

THE HOMELESS OF VENICE BEACH

1

THE HOMIE TOURIST

I stood facing the ocean, my heart pounding like the bass bin at a Rave. In front of me stretched the Santa Monica boardwalk. Palm trees swayed, seagulls frolicked; waves gently lapped up on the perfect shoreline.

"You better call me every morning by nine or I'm calling the cops!!" roared my roommate from her convertible VW Rabbit.

I adjusted the canvas bag on my shoulder, double-checked my baggy, non-descript outfit, and stuffed my long unruly hair up under a straw hat.

"I'm serious! People get raped, pillaged and looted down here!"

I turned and gave her a look. She snapped her mouth shut. We had only been roommates for a few months, but she was like the sister I never had. She had become my champion, educating me in the perils of Los Angeles. I was a refugee from Canada when we met at the L.A. Women in Film office. I was looking for an affordable room to rent. Her roommate had just moved out. Voila!

We found comfort and support in each other's company. We were both up to our writer's eyeballs in divorces. After one particularly vicious piece of correspondence from my Canadian albatross, we ceremoniously balled the letter up, set it on fire, and floated it out into the middle of the swimming pool. After a few martinis in the dying light of the Viking cremation I felt a whole lot better.

I had come from Canada, armed with my typewriter, guitar, and electric wok. I preferred not to wait around and see if my rampaging ex soul mate really could rip my intestines out through my nose. Every mile I put between me and the lawyers made me feel lighter, freer.

I fled to Los Angeles to live the dream; sell screenplays to Hollywood and live happily ever after. I should have been planning my next week of business meetings, doing lunch, getting connected. But after months of enduring meetings with producers operating on the aggressive side of charming I was disillusioned. At the end of each exasperating day, I would drive down to Venice Beach, befriend a homeless person, treat us to coffee and listen to their story. And they were GREAT stories.

As a writer, I became more and more at home with the homies, less and less comfortable with the "biz". My roommate wasn't impressed with the detour. One night as we were relaxing out by her kidney shaped pool in Burbank, she snapped. "Why don't you just go live with them and get it over with?"

A Stanley Cup sized epiphany slammed into my third eye. "That's it! You're right!"

"I was joking!"

"I'm not! I'm going!"

I was gleeful; she was panicked. And now I was standing on the edge of a cliff, ready to jump.

"Are you listening?" She scanned the beach nervously, looking for the homie who would be the end of me.

I tried one last time to calm her down. "Look, I traveled alone through Europe. Two months ago I was in the Yukon in a tent surrounded by 10,000 Grizzly Bears. How dangerous can this be? They're just people!"

Somehow, trying to explain my actions had become exhausting. I didn't know why I was doing this. I didn't know why this seemed like the life raft the Universe was tossing me.

"You have money! You have a place to live. People like you don't belong with the homeless."

I shrugged.

"Canadians!" she muttered. She threw her car into gear, waving her manicured hand in farewell as she sliced into the morning rush hour traffic, honking and flipping off her fellow motorists.

"And she thinks I'm crazy," I mused as I strolled onto the Santa Monica boardwalk.

The nearby Santa Monica Pier and its kaleidoscope of rides beckoned in the candy floss morning sun. But that wasn't the carnival I was looking for. I walked away from the Ferris wheel and headed toward the homeless.

I was raised by a wild mountain climber from the Yukon who had instilled a type of fearlessness in me that served me well during my lone travels around the world. When my father wasn't summiting a peak, he worked in construction, having the thankless job of supervising the trades on building sites. It was a stressful career, and his escape was the mountains.

He had a ritual upon attaining each summit. He would spread his arms, face the wind at the edge of the world and bellow, “Try and get me here ya bastards!”

I was feeling that way about divorce lawyers when I took my first steps onto the Santa Monica boardwalk. I tensed as the first test of the day approached me: a troop of grim-faced, homeless men. I had been dealing with the homeless one at a time until then. Intimidated, I looked away. Then that voice went off in my head. The one that had made me think this was a great idea in the first place.

“Oh, sure, go live with the homeless, but for God’s sake don’t talk to them.”

That internal smack upside the head to make me turn and look into the eyes of the lead male. I gave him my biggest smile. “Morning!”

“Morning pretty lady!” They all chimed back, grinning like kids at Christmas. “Have a great day!”

The sweetness of the response, the kindness that flowed out of them was touching. This just might work after all.

The sun was already scorching, and I wouldn’t last long if I didn’t take care of myself. I opened my father’s old canvas duffel bag and rummaged through it, looking for my sun screen. I pushed aside the grey army blanket, kiwi fruit, a change of underwear (Mom would be proud), notebooks, pens, my Swiss Army knife and twenty dollars. I found the sunscreen and smeared it onto my already sizzling façade.

My roommate was the only one who knew what I was doing. I didn't tell my family back in Canada, because frankly, I had no idea how to handle that kind of phone call.

"Hey, Mom? Oh, Los Angeles is great. Yup, weather's perfect. Nope, haven't met any movie stars yet cuz I'm living on the beach with the homeless."

I figured killing your folks with a phone call might go on the bad side of the karma check list.

I didn't know what was driving me, but I couldn't believe the purpose of life was to work to pay the bills. I wanted to believe that life was forgiving, and gracious, and a call to adventure. I said a silent prayer and prepared to exchange life as I knew it for something bigger.

*****

Santa Monica Beach lies directly north of Venice Beach. Both cities begrudgingly acknowledge that Los Angeles is nearby, but retain their separate identities.

Santa Monica is the sophisticated, intellectual sister to the wild, untamed Venice Beach sibling. Where Santa Monica seduces you with her beauty, her refinement, her rent controlled housing; Venice screams at you with a raw sexual energy that isn't accompanied by any kind of charm.

I decided to ease myself into this experiment by starting on Santa Monica beach.

After passing the men on the boardwalk, I relaxed into a slow, rhythmic walk. Closer to the ocean, weaving through the sand like a concrete serpent was the bike path. Rush hour was already in progress here with roller bladers, dog walkers, joggers and cyclists. I decided to play it safe and stay on the boardwalk in the slow lane with the elderly people with walkers.

I scanned the area for my next homie and quickly found him, a strikingly handsome black man with a beautiful smile. He was clean, dressed simply in a black shirt and pants. Only his shoes gave him away. The scuffed brown dress shoes had been worn into soft, slipper-like coverings held together with silver duct tape.

We started a casual conversation. I said I was visiting from Canada, and he immediately dubbed me, "Canada." He invited me to join his camp for pot luck at one of the picnic areas with a barbecue pit. I accepted.

His nickname was "Preacher". I guess he saw himself as leading his flock to redemption. The homeless always use nicknames. Birth names were for people living in boxes, filling out forms, always explaining themselves.

Well, the homeless were through with explaining their actions to anyone. They didn't care who I was, or what I'd done, they were only concerned with how I behaved. In a society where money was used to justify outrageous behavior, I liked this philosophy.

Preacher walked me over to his camp - 'camp' being a group of like-minded souls on similar journeys. As I was introduced to the group sitting at the picnic table it became clear this group of black men were felons fresh out of the penitentiary. Oh, great. I'd just wandered into the most dangerous camp on the beach.

Working hard to remain calm, I focused on making eye contact, and practicing the homie principle of watching how they behaved, not how they'd been labeled.

"Bunny", a diminutive, slender older man missing all but his front two teeth, grinned shyly at me like a child. What on Earth could he have been locked up for; timidity?

"Mumbles" circled me nervously, talking in one long, continuous thread, "You know you and me could get it on..."

They all laughed maniacally at him as he paced. Preacher whispered in my ear, "If you'd gone through what he did in the Pen, you'd be mumbling too."

Mumbles was dressed immaculately in a purple pant suit with flare bottoms and a purple paisley shirt. All that was missing was the mirror ball. Apparently, he had been arrested at a disco in the 70's.

Preacher seemed to be the spiritual centre of this camp, or lead con, I wasn't sure which. But he wasn't aggressive, and he had a protective air about him. So for the time being, I decided to trust him.

"Afro" didn't come over to be introduced. He stood at the barbecue, tending a pot of stew. He was a tall, rail thin man with a giant Afro hair style. Basketball was supposed to have been his ticket out of the ghetto. The drugs surrounding the court had unfortunately gotten him off track. Now he was a con with nowhere to go. He looked over his shoulder and glared at me.

Bunny took the opportunity to sneak up behind him, snatch a piece of meat off the barbecue and run.

Afro spun around and hollered after him. "You better get your crazy black ass back here before I knock you out."

Bunny crawled back, cowering before the Alpha male. Afro snatched back the meat, viciously chopped it up until it resembled road kill, then threw it in the pot.

Preacher explained, "Afro just got out a few days ago. He gonna be angry for while."

Being from the land of cowboys and the Calgary Stampede, I decided to follow the cowboy rule and keep my back to the wall, hand on my gun. Or in this case, back to the ocean; hand on my Swiss Army knife.

Normally it wasn't a big deal to me to walk up to a table of black men. My brother had nicknamed me "Minority Meg" in school because I dated Asians, Blacks, and any non-white within a hundred mile radius. I found them more interesting because their stories were so different from mine.

But this group was the most dangerous I'd ever wandered into. Within minutes of sitting down, two white cops on mountain bikes pulled up.

"Are you okay, Miss?"

With relief I realized my experiment had a safety net, there were cops everywhere.

"Yes, I'm fine thanks!"

I smiled at the police while the rest of my table looked guilty as hell. The cops peddled away, shooting warning glances at the camp.

I looked at my new friends, "You should try smiling at them next time."

The camp exploded with laughter; funny lady.

*****

The afternoon flew by, everyone trying to outdo the other with more and more outrageous stories. I laughed until I cried. I realized that during the dying years of my marriage, I had forgotten how to laugh. Ironically, these guys were the cure. I opened up my bag and pulled out two kiwi fruit.

"Anyone want some kiwi?"

They stared at me in wonder. It wasn't until years later when I was homeless with a toddler, that I realized what a magnanimous gesture this was. To pretend, just for a moment that we were friends on a day visit to the beach with all kinds of delicacies in a picnic basket, rather than strangers stranded in a dark night of the soul.

*****

As the sun set, the long awaited stew was finally ready to eat. We put together enough money to buy the high quality paper bowls that can hold hot meals. I think it was the best stew I had ever tasted. After a long day in the sun, eating only kiwi fruit, I was dangerously dehydrated and going into hypoglycemic shock. The stew saved me.

Word had spread down the shoreline that a "Homie Tourist" was at the Santa Monica camp. As darkness fell, ghostly apparitions began floating up the beach from Venice to check me out. Most glanced surreptitiously at me and passed on. Souls dressed in dark clothes melted in and out of the night. I was informed that white clothes were for rich people who can afford to clean them.

Once in a while, someone would try to sit next to me and chat. One man, an actor from Hollywood who came to the beach for drugs, slid in next to me on the bench. It was obvious he wanted to lure me away for sex. My camp saw what was happening. Within minutes he was unceremoniously tossed off the bench by Preacher and friends. I had become their pet, and no one was allowed to mess with me.

One man in particular caught my attention. He resembled Bob Marley, sporting long black dreadlocks decorated with all kinds of colorful beads and shiny objects. The lion's mane of dreads framed the eyes of Job. Colorful woven bags from Africa and Thailand hung off his body, bumping against his slender frame as he walked. He slid by like a ninja.

Bit by bit, some of the camp started to wander away, while others huddled closer to me. I looked at Bunny, his eyes popping out of his head, and realized he was more frightened than I was. The boundaries of prison didn't prepare them for this kind of freedom.

"Hey, Bunny, where's my guitar?" A monolithic black man appeared out of the night.

Bunny hopped, literally, in fear. "I g-g-g-gave it to D-D-D-DeBop."

The Monolith lifted Bunny off the bench by his collar. "You be confused. You want to get RID of something, give it to DeBop. You want a divorce;

leave your wife with DeBop. Come back, she be gone."

Wow, I should have left my husband with DeBop.

The group fell out laughing. The man lowered Bunny back onto the sand. "Now, why don't you go get my guitar?"

Bunny scurried off into the night as the beach morphed into something malignant. The cops on bicycles were coming by more often. Fights could be heard back in the alleys, random eruptions of screams bounced off the buildings and onto the beach.

"Miss, you really should go home," a cop in a cruiser warned me.

It was time for me to stop being the main attraction. I found Preacher and told him I was going to find a place to sleep. He spoke on behalf of his camp.

"You'll be safe if you lay your blankets here with us."

They all nodded somberly. I knew this group was capable of ending me. They hadn't been around a woman in years. But our day of sharing stories, laughter, and food had created trust, and in my heart I knew they would keep their word. They'd also watched me slice up the kiwi fruit with a Swiss Army knife. I had a weapon.

I smiled and thanked them. We agreed I should sleep under a palm tree near the water's edge, about one hundred yards off the frenzied activity of the boardwalk. I curled up in my Dad's old Army blanket, said a prayer of thanks, and immediately fell asleep.

*****

About two in the morning I was roughly shaken awake. "Canada! Oh, Canada!"

Much giggling followed this. I pried open my eyes. They better not be singing my national anthem to me. The camp had gone on a bender and the troops were visibly drunk.

"We got you a *Fat Boy Burger*!!" They proudly rammed the squished shark bait under my nose.

"Thanks, guys. Maybe later."

"NO! Now! With us!" A sea of ridiculously eager faces stared at me. I relented and struggled up to a sitting position. We opened the wrappings of the oozing, monstrous burgers. Most of mine dripped onto the sand, but somehow I crammed the rest into my mouth. After this quick pit stop, the camp rumbled off, stumbling up the shoreline, laughing, falling down, electrified to be alive and free.

Meanwhile, the Fat Boy Burger staged a coup d'état on my brain. After several un-ladylike belches and rumbles of protest from my stomach, I gave up on sleep. I leaned against the palm tree and stared at the sky.

The immensity of the heavens seemed to be sitting right on top of me. Shooting stars streaked across the night sky. Otherworldly lights danced in the heavens then vanished. I realized this was why my dad climbed mountains; to find peace with the universe away from mankind's influence.

I pondered the irony of life. I'd just spent the day with one of the most dangerous groups of people imaginable, and had been treated with great care and respect. The people society claimed I should be with, the well dressed white guys in boardrooms, were the perverted, dangerous ones. One notorious producer in Hollywood expected people to sit through meetings with him while his balls, carefully shoved out through his zipper, were being licked by his Chihuahua. Where's that Tazer Gun when you really need it?

I was turning my back on a life that had disappointed at every turn. I was constantly baffled by other people's ability to follow the pack, even if it meant leading lives of quiet desperation.

I took in my new reality: the Pacific Ocean in front of me, and the crazed sampling of humanity behind me. Eerie noises echoed off the buildings. The lullaby of crack heads fighting drifted up from Venice. The voices were no longer human, more like something from a horror movie using voice processors and special effects.

I huddled against my palm tree and pulled the blanket closer. I hoped the grey covering would make me invisible. Dark shapes approached but they were too busy fighting to see me. This was why people feared the beach at night. Drug addicts who hadn't slept or eaten for weeks were moving Zombie-like, eyes stretched wide open and crazed. Their flesh cascaded off their emaciated frames, cooked to perfection under the blazing California sun.

Finally the sky began to lighten up, the approaching dawn chasing the night creatures back into their hiding places. I had officially made it through my first night. Mist covered the beach, giving it a mystical feel. I gathered my things and walked over to the washrooms. They were locked up tight.

"Only tourists are allowed to use them," said a voice behind me.

I turned to see Afro on a bench, hands clenched, head down, the way basketball players sit on the bench after being fouled out of a game. I looked around nervously. We were alone. But his mood had changed, his anger gone. I sat down next to him.

"You sleep okay?" I asked lamely.

He shook his head. "Couldn't sleep with all that racket."

We sat for awhile in silence. I'd learned homies don't like chatterboxes, so I waited.

"You know, when I was in the Pen, I got clean; didn't do drugs or alcohol for eight years." He stared at his hands as he spoke. "First day out, I was right back doing everything I wanted to get away from; drugs, booze. Seeing you yesterday, listening to you, made me realize how much I missed a woman's company. Not just for sex, but the way you say things, the way you put a lid on everyone's crazy. We all behaved cuz a you. I don't wanna get back in the old mix. I never wanted to end up like this. I wanted to get married, have kids."

That's when I finally saw him, the young basketball player who could have ended up playing against my own brother; the person he had been before he was locked up.

"Well," I started slowly, choosing my words carefully, "I think you've got to get away from here. Get a job downtown in a mailroom or something. Then, women will get used to seeing you, and get to know you."

He shook his head. "I never been good at dating."

"No one is! Everyone's uncomfortable and shy and afraid of being turned down!"

He stared at me in disbelief. "Even you?"

"Dating's the worst!"

A soft smile spread across his face. I had just solved one of the mysteries of the Universe.

"Get a job where you can be around women, then, if you like someone, ask her out for coffee; nothing scary about coffee."

We grinned at each other. Just two friends talking, no police for miles.

"Where are you going next?" he asked.

"Venice Beach."

He shook his head, serious again. "I wouldn't go there if I was you. I'm even scared of Venice."

"That's where I'm supposed to be." I tied my runners together and looped them through my duffel bag strap. My bare feet practically giggled at the feel of the wet sand. Growing up in -40 degree winters makes walking barefoot a luxury.

I looked at him one last time. "You take care of yourself."

"Thank you, for taking the time, to talk to me." As I walked away, he became the mist.

2

WELCOME TO VENICE BEACH

Venice Beach, California, was the brain child of Tobacco millionaire Abbot Kinney in 1905. He bought two miles of ocean front property south of Santa Monica in 1891 and proceeded to build canals to drain the marshland. He loved the old world charm of Venice, Italy, and wanted to recreate it in America. He would probably roll over in his grave to know it was now called "Dog Town", and home to the pioneering skateboarders, the "Z-Boys".

The Venice Boardwalk, officially Ocean Front Walk, hosts a kaleidoscope of brightly painted low rise buildings on the east side, giving it a quaint beach town feel. Tall, majestic palm trees interspersed with homie craftsmen line the west side. You can find everything from jewelry to a chiropractic adjustment on the rent free side of the boardwalk.

I stopped in front of the *Sidewalk Café* with its inviting red and white awning. Last week I was a regular here for coffee. Today I was one of the homeless. I stared longingly in the window of its neighbor, *Small World Books*. This building had actually been home to poets, including Jack Kerovac (*On the Road*), in the sixties. Venice had been a haven, and muse, for creative souls for decades.

Suzanne, the woman behind the famous Leonard Cohen song, lived in her camper and danced for tourists on Venice Beach. As I walked along the boardwalk I recognized many famous faces, especially stand up comics, down here doing research, looking for inspiration and enjoying the day.

I carried on past the *Pacific Jewish Centre*, fondly called "The Shul on the Beach." This cheery yellow synagogue had been holding Saturday services for sixty years at the same location.

Across from these buildings were henna tattoo stands, incense vendors, and displays of Indian deities. I tried to blend in with the homies rather than the tourists. This subtle shift in my energy attracted the inner circle of nut jobs that fuel the Venice Beach engine.

Within two hours of mingling on the Venice boardwalk I was offered a job riding elephants in the circus. A few steps further along I was confronted with a young Born-Again-Christian kid who was waiting for God to save him from the street. His jeans hung off bony hips, and his Grateful Dead tie-died t-shirt had more red on it than usual. I think it was blood. He was so gaunt and dehydrated I gave him some kiwi fruit. I told him I was sure God wouldn't mind if he ate something while he was waiting to be saved. He started to cry.

His situation reminded me of a joke I once heard: a man in the mountains slips and falls off a cliff. He manages to grab a branch jutting out from the rock. As he dangles hundreds of feet above a deep ravine he prays, "Please, God, if you really exist, help me!"

A deep thundering voice answers, "I am here, my son. Surrender, let go of the branch."

The man takes a deep breath and yells again, "Anybody else up there?"

*****

Venice is called "Dog Town" because everyone brings their dogs to the beach and lets them run free. No one picks up after them. Combine that with the locked washrooms at night and the place smells like a urinal.

I passed a juggler doing his act with a chain saw, a bowling ball, and a golf club. I half expected a flaming torch to appear out of his ass. Dizzily I backed away from the crowd and was almost run over by Harry Perry, arguably the most famous busker in town. Dressed all in white, complete with turban, and shin pads, he was blissfully playing his red and white bull's eye electric guitar, on roller blades. He sailed through the crowd like a vision.

I made my way over to a pay phone and dutifully called my roommate at her office. She was working in the thick of the film industry. Her dream of becoming a writer had been sidetracked when the producers she worked for realized she could do accounting; a talent worth its weight in gold here. So, she ended up doing the kind of job she could have done back in Oklahoma.

She picked up on the first ring. "Where are you? Are you alright? What's happening down there?"

"I'm great, I'm fine. It's a beautiful day."

"That's it?"

"What? You're disappointed?"

She backtracked and mumbled some words of encouragement before hanging up. I was confused. It felt as if she wanted harm to come to me; proof that her view of the world was correct. Well, nothing I could do about that. I pondered this as my dried out tongue began to stick to the roof of my sandblasted mouth.

If I didn't find some water fast I'd wind up all woozy like yesterday.

I wandered over to a concession stand and almost tripped over a pile of rags. A dazzling blue eye peeked out at me. "Got a light?"

A man's upper torso emerged from the rags; his only hand held a crinkled cigarette butt. I felt the world shift slightly beneath my feet. This wasn't what a human being was supposed to look like in America; maybe in a war torn country, but not here.

"Sorry, I don't smoke." We stared at each other a moment. "What happened to you?" I finally blurted out.

He sighed, and using his one arm, shifted his weight slightly. "I was a heavy equipment operator. There was an accident. Both my legs and one arm were torn off. Turned out the company didn't have insurance, so here I am."

I couldn't believe what I was hearing. Coming from Canada with nationalized health care, I was speechless. How many people here had been tossed away like fast food wrappers? I pulled a couple of dollars out of my pocket and pressed them into his hand.

"Take care of yourself." I mumbled. He nodded and disappeared back into his nest. I moved away from him, my head spinning, wondering where to go next when a balled up human being came flying down a set of stairs, landing at my feet. I was so startled I screamed and jumped back.

The homie at my feet unraveled and jumped to his feet, laughing. He was a small, slender man, dressed in rags, a braided beard dangling from his chin. He bowed low. A round of applause came from the homeless cheering section sitting on the sand, watching the performance. Apparently I had just walked onto the set of “Homie TV”.

I smiled weakly and waved at the crowd. They cheered at my good nature as I stumbled away. By noon I was exhausted. I wasn’t used to being around so many emotionally wrecked people. It was like being stuck in the mall during the Christmas rush. I bought myself a sandwich and a bottle of water. I spotted some benches away from the boardwalk and made a beeline for them. Sitting in the shade of a pagoda, eating, calmed my nerves. I closed my eyes and let the ocean breeze clear my head.

Maybe I really was deluded. How could I survive here for a week if the first thirty hours had drained me this badly?

“Hey, didn’t I see you last night?”

I looked up. A figure was standing in front of me, the sun silhouetting him along with the palm trees.

“Pardon me?”

He plopped down on the bench across from me. “The Santa Monica camp, I saw you there.” It was the Bob Marley ninja I had seen the night before; the one with the amazing eyes. I relaxed.

“Sure, I remember you. It was pretty crazy up there.”

“Yeah, those cons be trippin’ for real. You stay up there last night?”

“Yup.”

He raised an eyebrow.

“They were okay,” I said.

“That’s a dangerous camp. I’m scared a them.”

“Funny, that’s what they said about Venice.”

We grinned at each other. In the sunlight I could see he was a slender man with long, elegant hands. He had on black dress pants worn shiny from overuse as ‘beach wear’, a crew neck sweater, and worn Keds on his feet.

And he loved his jewelry. His left ear displayed an earring in the shape of Africa; several other plain small hoops adorned the right. He was wearing a collection of hand-made beaded necklaces. The ensemble was finished off with many shiny objects and feathers woven into his dreadlocks. Like a crow, he had decorated his nest with treasures. His nest just happened to sit on his head. Years later, I saw a picture of the Hindu God Shiva who looked just like him.

“Want to come hang with my camp? It’s right over here.”

He pointed to a mound of sand surrounded by three palm trees. A scattering of young men in their late teens and early twenties were lounging on the sand. It was a tranquil oasis compared to the boardwalk.

“Sure, why not.”

He put out his hand. “They call me Rasta.”

“I’m …”

“Canada. I heard.”

We joined his camp in the shade under the palm trees. “Rikki”, a Latino teenager dressed in a bright orange ski jacket and cardboard stiff jeans was standing, lecturing, while the young men on the ground giggled and nudged each other. I looked questioningly at Rasta and he whispered in my ear, “He’s schizophrenic.”

“Junior”, a good looking, well-muscled black teenager grinned at me and pointed to Rikki. “He’s just made a bold hypothesis, and he’s waiting for the applause to die down.”

Sitting next to Junior was “David”, the human incarnation of Michelangelo’s David. I had never seen a more perfect looking human in my life. His body was perfectly sculpted, golden white blond curls framed his chiseled face, electric blue eyes glanced lazily over at me. Only the scars running up both arms hinted at something darker going on.

This was Rikki’s audience, at least, the one I could see. But Rikki was seeing a much grander view. He smiled and stared off at a sea of people in another dimension. Sweat poured down his face. He gestured and mumbled, then nodded as if listening to the responses.

The temperature was in the 80s, and he was in a down-filled jacket; part of his weight loss strategy I suppose. He finally staggered into the shade and shed the jacket, his moment in the spotlight over. His T-shirt was soaked and plastered to his slender frame. Rasta pulled an extra tank top out of a bag and helped Rikki exchange it for the dry one.

I was mesmerized. What did Rikki’s reality look like? Did it touch on mine at all? I had been doing research on a piece titled “Schizophrenia vs. Mysticism”, but could only find Mystics to interview. Mentally ill people like Rikki had been released from hospitals due to lack of funding. I had inadvertently stumbled onto a live subject. “You take care of him?” I asked Rasta.

He shrugged and gestured at his camp, “We all do.” He sat down on a faded orange batik cloth that was spread out on the sand. The corners were weighted down against the ocean breeze by his colorful backpacks and books. He motioned for me to have a seat.

“Welcome to the Sandominium,” giggled Junior.

There was a grace, and a joy, about this group that I hadn’t found with the others. Junior opened up a copy of Kahlil Gibran’s *The Prophet* and read. Rikki hummed and drew in the sand. Rasta pulled out some yarn and began crocheting a circular pattern out of red, gold and green.

“What are you crocheting?”

“Crowns for dreads.” He showed me a stack of finished oversized berets worn by men with dreadlocks to keep their hair clean. He grabbed one and stuffed his dreads up into it, then bobbed his head around to let everything settle into place. He tossed one over to me. “Here, try one.”

I took off my hat and put the crocheted piece on my head like a tam. The camp giggled. Rasta took it and gently stuffed my hair up into it.

“See, it will keep your hair from getting split ends and bleaching out in the sun.”

As if on cue, two men with long dreadlocks walked over and squatted down in front of him. They wore brilliant red, gold, and green tunics over black pants, and sandals. Each one carried a drum.

“Give praise and thanks, Brother. Fine crowns,” said one with faint hints of grey in his beard.

“One love”, replied Rasta.

They each picked up a crown. “R-R-R-Rastafar-I!” growled the taller, younger man appreciatively.

Rasta smiled, happy for the complement.

“Irie. Would *I* allow to try?” asked the other.

I was having trouble following the conversation. I had never been exposed to the Rastafarian culture. They could have been speaking Swahili for all I knew. Rasta nodded and the two Jamaicans each took a crown and pushed their dreadlocks up inside. They tossed their heads, the crowns held tight.

“Did the *I* make the crowns?” asked the tall man.

“Ya mon,” said Rasta, “my mother taught me when she was sick with cancer. Maybe teaching a fool like me kept her alive.”

“True,” they replied.

“Now the *I* survives making crowns for Jah Rastafari.”

“What the *I* ask for the crown?” asked the elder man.

“Hey I gotta get my fifteen dollars. But for Rasta? Donations.”

Each man passed him a twenty dollar bill. The elder with the grey in his beard discreetly handed him a joint as well. “Ites to partake in.”

Rasta slid the money into his pocket, the marijuana into his Ked runner. “Give praise and thanks.” He held up the index finger of his right hand and said the Rastafarian blessing. “One love, brothers, one love.”

They responded in kind and moved away. Rasta pulled out a five. "Junior, go get us some wheat grass for lunch."

Junior took the five dollar bill and sauntered away with David. Rikki seemed happy, sitting so close to me, yet light years away.

"Why do you say *I and I*?" I asked Rasta.

"Babylon," he waved his hand indicating Los Angeles, "forced a corrupt language on our ancestors when they were brought here from Africa. We take negative words and make them positive, *I* instead of *me*, because *me* is an object, insinuating a victim, whereas *I* is the subject. *I and I* shows our oneness with God, Jah, the Most High."

When he spoke to me, he sounded like a university professor. He changed his dialect at will, a societal chameleon. It was a gift, reflecting people back on themselves; making anyone he spoke to feel comfortable.

I watched as he started crocheting a new crown. His long fingers worked effortlessly with the yarn. He had the delicate touch that comes from years of practice. It reflected his inner calmness. My past attempts at knitting or crocheting always resulted in a tightly wound mass resembling something a cat would cough up. Funny, of the two of us, the homeless guy was the peaceful one.

Rikki was subtly edging his way closer to me until we were sitting side by side. He mumbled softly and gestured with his hands. I noticed with alarm that some of his fingers had been cut off at the first and second joints. His energy was soft, like a puppy. Every once in a while he would laugh a light, childlike laugh. I couldn't help but laugh every time he did. We sat like this for a long time; giggling at the sun, the world, our mismatched realities.

David and Junior returned with several one ounce containers of wheat grass.

“Where’s your shirt?” demanded Rasta of the now shirtless Junior.

“Sold it for a buck.”

“To who?”

“Guy with a buck.”

“Don’t bring your weepy, sunburned ass around me tonight.”

They laughed and passed the wheat grass around, including one for me.

“Oh, no, guys, this is your lunch,” I protested.

“Not if you join the camp.” Rasta looked at me, deep inside me. “You’ll be safe if you lay your blankets here.”

“This is the one you’ve been looking for,” whispered the voice in my head.

I felt strange rushes of energy moving through me. I didn’t know I was looking for a homeless black guy. My understanding of reality was shifting, and I didn’t know what to do.

They shot back their wheat grass as if they were at the bar of some exotic Jamaican resort. I eyed my tiny plastic cup of green goo suspiciously. Rasta realized I needed some encouragement.

“Ann Wigmore discovered the healing powers of wheat grass. She was given six months to live and remembered a passage in the Bible saying "eat the grasses of the field". She found wheat grass had the most nutrients, started juicing and drinking it, and cured herself. Now she treats people abandoned by the medical profession at her institute. Try it, it's what keeps us healthy, and it only costs half a buck."

I chugged back the liquid, cringed, did a little shiver, and smiled a big green smile at the crew. They smiled back green in reply.

"Give praise and thanks," said Rasta quietly. I was beginning to understand what he meant.

*****

The day passed like a dream. I was completely unaware of the crowds and commotion going on behind us. All I was aware of was the slender, dreadlocked man in front of me. He sat under the three palms, the rest of us around him in a half circle. His compassion seemed boundless, his joy at the smallest blessings in life immense. I felt as if I had fallen up the rabbit hole, out of my fantasy life, and into reality. I was at peace.

"What the fuck are you staring at!!" roared a loud British She Devil.

I whirled around. A huge pregnant British woman in her twenties was thundering toward us. Her shirt was unbuttoned, trailing her like a cape, while her massive pendulous breasts rocked and rolled. Her "baby-on-board" belly glistened and rolled beneath them. The boobs and belly were sunburned. Her blond dye job had grown out to reveal a black streak across the top of her head. Lovely.

I looked at my camp. They stared at the sand, careful not to look at her. They'd obviously dealt with her before.

"I said what the fuck..."

A small, nervous hippie tried in vain to control her. He was one of those pale, skinny guys who would have looked better with his head shaved. His long wispy hair was almost invisible. "Please, honey, come back. Your shirt..."

He tried in vain to pull the shirt closed around her naked torso. She swatted him away like Godzilla swinging at airplanes atop the Empire State Building. She glared at the camp, itching for a fight. But the sun was burning her pallid complexion, the hippie relentless in trying to cover her up. She finally gave in and let herself be led away.

"Couldn't be crazy in her own country, had to come here and lose it." Rasta shook his head.

"That Crazy Brit is getting on my nerves," mumbled Junior.

I sat there with my mouth open, speechless. I could honestly say I had never seen a pregnant woman behave quite like that. The look on my face gave the camp the giggles.

Rasta shook his head. "Ain't she a trip?"

I nodded dumbly.

"Welcome to Venice," said David.

They all exchanged high fives except for Rikki who thought they were waving goodbye and got smacked in the head.

*****

It was five o'clock and David and Junior were making dinner plans. Shirtless Junior was now quite sunburned.

"But if we leave now, we can get to Hill Street in time for dinner."

"But this girl I met today said to drop by and eat at her place."

"But Hill Street is a sure thing!"

Rasta shook his head. "You know, they be arguing clear through dinner, then come whining to me cuz they're hungry. It's like a body where every arm, leg and organ has its own opinion. Just like America, so in time of crisis, it can't make a decision, it just blows the fuck up."

He packed up his bags. "Time for my runnins."

"Your what?" I asked, once again, having trouble keeping up with the street slang.

"My runnins; the daily occupations with which I occupies myself," he grinned at me. "Want to come?"

"Sure". I had nowhere else to go.

"Better put your shoes on," he warned.

"I like walking barefoot!"

"Barefoot's for people who stay at a hotel with a medic. You're on the street. You get a nail or a splinter in your foot you'll be hobbled. You depend on your feet for survival out here; better take care of them."

He wiggled his toes inside his worn Keds. "These puppies of mine haven't seen daylight for years."

I put my runners on. "Can we eat something first?"

He nodded and we walked to a small Mexican restaurant on the boardwalk. "She has a dollar plate for homies. You need some money?"

"I'm good," I said, pulling out a buck.

We ordered and received paper plates piled with beans, rice, salsa and a soft tortilla. We smiled and thanked her. She gave us both big smiles and continued cooking for her packed restaurant.

"Some people got heart," said Rasta.

We watched the sun set as we ate. The sky above the calm ocean faded to a deep indigo blue. The silhouettes of the palm trees stood guard against the coming night. With food in me I was feeling calmer, ready to experience "runnins".

We moved off the boardwalk and into a pitch black alley. I stayed close as we passed clusters of men huddled in groups. Whenever they saw Rasta they'd nod a greeting.

"Where are we going?" I spoke in a hushed voice.

"Gotta see the Jamaican. I'm doing cover art for his next album."

"You're an artist?"

"Yup."

I was excited. One of my best friends in Canada was an artist and for awhile I sold her paintings while I was trying to figure my life out. I loved being around the art community, it inspired me.

"Don't sound so excited, most of us die homeless or missing an ear," he said quietly.

"So, what kind of things do you do?"

"Concert posters, T-shirts, you name it. In Atlantic City I did portraits on the boardwalk. There was a line of us artists competing with each other, so I had to catch the tourists' attention. I wore a hand-painted cowboy hat, did the portraits upside down."

"You were upside down?" I knew it was a stupid question but I was dizzy from heat stroke and the alley was spinning.

"No," he said patiently, as if I was his slightly inbred cousin. "I'd start at the bottom of the page, with the top of their head, and move up."

We exited the alley onto a street. The dim street lights were a welcome relief after the eerie darkness.

He drew an invisible portrait in the air. "When I finished, I'd turn it upright and it would be perfect. I had a line of customers waiting on me."

He smiled at the memory. But it quickly left. Old memories sometimes cause pain, especially if they were good ones that couldn't be recaptured. We moved down the street and into another dark alley.

"So, how long you been curbed?" he asked.

"Curbed?" I repeated. Again, the idiot cousin.

"On the curb, street, homeless, without visible means of support," he said patiently.

"Oh, just since yesterday."

"Wasn't for anything funky was it, like Hair-on, or crack?" He looked sideways at me.

"Hair-on?" I sighed.

“We’re gonna need an interpreter here soon. Hair-on, Heroin, cuz if you’re doin’ smack or anything funky, you belong with the slammers back there.”

“No, I hate drugs. And what do you mean, I belong with them?”

“Homies peep you out for twenty-four hours, see if you’re The Man.” He saw my confused look and went slower. “See if you’re an undercover cop, see what your story is. The camp you belong to invites you to join.”

Gee, just like being rushed into a sorority. “So, why did you invite me to your camp?”

“All the homeboys in our camp are runaways. Got the feeling you’re running away from something, Canada.”

We turned a corner and almost ran smack into a screaming trio. An older woman bellowed at her teenage daughter. “You ain’t nothin’ but a human vending machine, twenty dollars a trick, twenty dollars for crack, all day, all night!”

“Leave her alone,” snarled the girl’s brother.

“Don’t tell me what to do, Motherfucker!”

“I ain’t never fucked you.”

She smacked him so hard the sound echoed off the buildings. The woman was spiraling out of control. Rasta moved in quickly.

“Hey, you’re gettin’ too far out there. You wanna bring the Rollers down on us?”

The mother shook her head.

"Then chill," commanded the homie referee. We moved on. Rasta let out a huge sigh. "They ought a quit. Mother's a slammer, and she's trying to pull rank on her babies. That sure is fucked up."

"Slammer?"

"Heroin addict."

Funny how easy it is to take your parents for granted until you witness a scene like that. No matter how tough things got, even when Dad lost his business and had my two widowed grandmothers to support plus us kids, Mom and Dad never took it out on us. They both went to work, and I'd hear them laughing at night when we were all in bed, keeping each other's morale up.

Stumbling on that warm fuzzy scene in the alley sure smacked some gratitude into my fat, self-centered head. I remembered feeling neglected because I had the only working Mom in the neighborhood. Good thing I wasn't coming home to find her strung out on heroin, turning tricks. I really would have been a whiner.

"What are Rollers?" I asked, adding to my Street Thesaurus.

"Cops in cars."

We turned a corner and headed down an even darker alley. I hoped my instincts about him were right because I didn't have a hope in hell of finding my way back to the beach.

We walked up to a non-descript building with a metal door. Rasta knocked softly.

"Just a minute," sang a voice from a nearby barred window. We stood patiently; nothing.

Rasta knocked again and whispered loudly, “Hey, man, open up!”

“Just a minute,” said the voice again.

I went over and peeked in the window. A parrot on a perch stared back. It cocked its head at me, deciding if I was edible.

“Just a minute!” it squawked.

“It’s a bird,” I giggled. “Maybe you should knock louder.

Rasta was irritated. “Homies don’t do nothin’ loud. Draws too much attention. Don’t run, don’t yell, just try to be invisible.” He put his face closer to the door. “Come on man, it’s me, Rasta.”

“Ya, Mon, hold your horses,” drawled a deep, velvety voice behind the door. It cracked open. Pot smoke billowed out through the doorway. Rasta took a deep, appreciative inhale. Standing there was the “Jamaican”; a striking, middle aged Dread. He had an athletic build and the presence that comes from years of performing on stage. He was floating in a cloud of marijuana, and he seemed confused to see us.

“You asked me to come over. Said you wanted me to do some cover art,” Rasta reminded the incredibly high musician.

“Oh, ya, right.” The Jamaican continued to block the door and gave me the once over. “Who ‘dis?” he mumbled.

Rasta ignored him and walked into the living room. The Jamaican blocked my way. He wanted my street ID.

“I’m his roadie.”

He smirked and he let me enter. What used to be a living room was now a rehearsal hall and store room. Every inch of space was filled with musical instruments, sound equipment, and trash. The Jamaican's Reggae Concert posters filled the walls.

I turned to Rasta, "You did these?"

He nodded, "All of them."

The art was stunning, original. Rasta should have been making a fortune in an ad agency somewhere. Instead, he was prowling back alleys in the dark looking for work.

The Jamaican signaled for us to follow him into the kitchen. He sat down at the kitchen table where a scale was set up and piles of marijuana were waiting to be weighed. Several Hollywood actors stood around, sharing a large cigar-shaped spliff. I recognized one of them as the man who tried to get me away from the camp in Santa Monica. Ah yes, the glamour of Tinsel town.

The haze floating near the ceiling in the kitchen created a giant bong; not a smoke detector in sight. Rasta tried in vain to hurry the heavily sedated proceedings along. "You figure out what artwork you want?"

The Jamaican gave us a lazy once over, "Where's your boyfriend, da Poet?" He sucked on the spliff in slow motion, enjoying it like a fine Cuban cigar. Smoke curled up through his dreadlocks and around his face.

"Come on, man, don't do me like this." Rasta shook his head, tired of the game.

The Jamaican stood up and roughly bumped into me as he made his way past, copping a feel as he moved by.

I was wedged between the fridge and the counter, and had nowhere to go. He grinned and floated into the bedroom. Any other time, I would have kneed him in the balls. But this wasn't my business meeting, and I didn't want to make things worse for Rasta. I moved closer to the living room, ready to escape. I didn't even smoke cigarettes, and the room was making me light-headed.

The Jamaican returned with a pale, fragile looking teenage girl following him. She was wearing one of the Jamaican's concert T-shirts like a mini dress and looked even higher than the men. The Jamaican handed a piece of paper to Rasta.

"Indigo drew 'dis. Is what I and I want."

Rasta took the drawing and stared at it. "Aw, shit," he said under his breath.

I looked over his shoulder at the childish drawing. There was no joy in Rasta's voice when he spoke. "So, you want this?"

"Just like 'dat; my name in red, gold and green. You know, and de portrait."

The Jamaican gave him a cold stare and slid his hand up under Indigo's T-shirt. He was old enough to be her grandfather, and according to the new homie rules I had learned, I did not like the way he was behaving. I didn't give a rat's ass who he thought he was, Mr. "I and I" was repulsive.

"Which portrait?" Any hope of Rasta being inspired by this project was quickly evaporating.

The Jamaican pointed to the one on Indigo's T-shirt.

"You still have the original artwork I did for you?"

The Jamaican shook his head "no" and reached over to a poster on the wall and ripped it off. He handed it over and continued fondling the young girl.

"I need money for art supplies." Rasta's tenacity amazed me.

"Come back tomorrow, I give it to you then," said the spider to the fly.

"Come on, man, you know you got the money now."

"Tomorrow," the Jamaican grunted. He turned to me. "You can come by anytime."

The actors smirked, Indigo crawled onto his lap.

Rasta leaned close to the Jamaican, "Whatever you're thinking, she's not the one."

I was out the front door and down the alley before I realized I had no idea where I was. I waited for Rasta to catch up, and we moved silently through the dark.

I didn't speak to him until we were back on Ocean Front Walk. "I think I better go."

"You're trippin'."

"What?" My temper had reached boiling point.

"You're upset, you're trippin', what is it?"

"I don't do drugs, and if you do, I'm out of here." I was tired of "Busy Guys"; coked out guys, slammin' guys, guys who stay up all night rustling around your place being busy. You wake up in the morning and find them in your closet trying on your underwear. I'd had enough of it in the oil patch in Canada and I wasn't in the mood for it here.

"That punk Jamaican, why'd he do me like that?"

"Forget about him. Who's the Poet? Is he your drug dealer? How many drugs do you do?" I was starting to yell. He gave me a look, silently reminding me I was a homie now, and homies don't make a scene. I shut up. He spoke quietly, soothingly.

"Jah gave me herb, healing of a nation. It's what keeps me from putting a brick through that knucklehead's skull." His large, compassionate eyes pleaded with me to understand.

I ignored the look, I was angry. "I've been in lots of situations that were hard, but I got through them without doing drugs."

"You ever been a homeless black Vietnam Vet?"

He had me there. I had no idea what he was going through. I was so out of my comfort zone I felt like the Earth's tectonic plates were shifting under my feet. He watched me with weary eyes. "Put your bag down."

"What?" No one was taking my bag, it was all I had.

"Trust me."

I reluctantly put the bag down.

"Do this."

He began spinning clockwise in a graceful twirling motion, right hand extended up to the stars, left hand pointed at the earth. I took a deep breath and self-consciously did the same. Within three rotations I felt lighter, freer. It was as if the spinning shook off the weirdness of the past few hours. Eventually we stopped and smiled sadly at each other.

He headed to a nearby bench. "Come on."

I followed and plunked down next to him. "I need to sleep," I whined. My head was spinning from dehydration, exhaustion, and my new found high, complements of the Jamaican.

"Not yet."

Damn this homelessness was exhausting! I thought everyone just hung around doing nothing. At a loss for what to do while we waited, I kept talking. "So, how many drugs have you done?"

"Just enough. I went through art school on acid, but that was the Sixties. You get the same revelations from a cheap two dollar hit of acid as you do from fifteen years of meditation. The difference is meditation stays with you."

A police cruiser, correction "Rollers", moved slowly towards us on the boardwalk, shining a bright spotlight at the beach. As it came abreast of us it stopped. The two policemen stared at us, we stared back. No one spoke.

My Canadian manners tried to pry my mouth open and say something charming, but I could tell this wasn't the time. Finally, they moved away, shining the spotlight back on the beach, looking for homies. The place was deserted save for us. The cruiser got to the end of the boardwalk and turned up Rose, the borderline for Venice. Finally, we had a break. Before we could move another cruiser entered the boardwalk from the opposite direction.

"Damn!" Rasta was becoming just as frustrated.

So was I. I needed to lie down. "That young girl, Indigo, why would her parents allow her to be with the Jamaican?"

"You're talking like her parents give a damn. Where do you think all these young kids come from? You think they're curbed because it's worse than being home? No, it's better. Look at David. He should be the captain of the football team, dating the prom queen, right?"

I had to agree, David was gorgeous.

"His momma started molesting him when he was a child. All those scars on his arms are suicide attempts. Finally, he ran away, landed here on the beach. Snuck home one night to get some clothes and she called the police, had him arrested for break and enter. SHE abuses HIM, and he gets arrested over a pile of clothes. She ought a quit."

"That's insane!"

"Hello."

"And what about Rikki's fingers?"

Rasta moved to the edge of his seat, ready to move. "Voices keep telling him to cut them off."

The last patrol car cleared the boardwalk.

"Let's do it!" Rasta jumped up with his bags and sprinted across the sand toward the ocean. He moved lightly, like a gazelle. I thundered behind him like an earth mover; large wheels, no grace. Each step I took I sunk deep into the sand. He skimmed ahead of me into the distance, the moonlit ocean in front of him.

"Where are we going?" I hissed.

"Inside the wall."

He gestured to a stand of logs that had been sunk into the ground forming a small wall. He dropped down on the ocean side. I stumbled up next to him and fell to the sand panting.

He shook his head at my condition. "You said you were an athlete."

"Cold weather, hard ground athlete," I wheezed.

Rasta began digging in the sand at our feet. He linked his hands and used his hands and arms like a giant scoop.

"What are you doing?"

"This is where we're sleeping. You're there." He pointed to a spot a few feet away. Following his lead, I started scooping out a shallow trench. Rasta had several blankets and a plastic tarp buried in the sand. He pulled them out and kept working, looking around the wall at the boardwalk every few seconds.

"Stop!" He crouched behind the wall of logs. I dropped next to him. The spotlight from the police cruiser shot across the sand to the ocean.

"Aren't we allowed to be here?"

"It's illegal to sleep on the beach."

I guess the previous night the Santa Monica cops were so busy trying to keep up with the cons partying up and down the beach; they didn't notice me curled up under the palm tree.

Rasta swiftly completed his trench, and lined it with the tarp.

"Is the rest of your camp here somewhere?"

"I'm the only one that sleeps this way. They call me Dead Man. Being buried spooks them out too much."

Wait. Buried? We were going to be buried? He placed three heavy wool blankets in the trench.

"Who is The Poet that the Jamaican asked you about?"

"He's part of the camp; a writer, like you. You'll probably meet him tomorrow at the *Breakfast Club.*"

His nest was finished. I had barely created a pothole. He scooted over next to me and used the same scooping method with his arms to create my trench. I pulled out my grey army blanket.

He eyed it skeptically. "That's all you got?"

"It's summer, I'll be fine."

He shrugged and pulled off his shoes and hid them under the blankets. He used one of his bags as a pillow and lay down. I followed his example and stretched out in the sand. He covered himself with a blanket, then proceeded to scoop sand over himself. He motioned for me to do the same. I scooped sand onto my lone blanket and faced him. All that was visible of him now was his head. He was facing me, a small passage near his face let air in. He pulled the blankets over his head and vanished from sight. I did the same, and immediately started giggling.

"Shhh!"

A helicopter was coming up the coastline, its huge spotlight searching the beach for, well, us. I stayed still, the light passed over us and continued up the beach.

"This is like the movie *Blade Runner*!" I giggled, picturing myself as a synthetic human running from the law. "That helicopter didn't see us?"

"From the air we look like abandoned beach blankets. They're looking for bumps," explained my homie tour guide.

"I love camping!" I babbled.

He finally peeked out at me, since I wouldn't shut up.

"Camping? I'm an army brat. Can't say I ever went camping. Grew up in Philly, New York, Kansas City. No wilderness. Aren't there predators out there... camping?"

"Sure, but back home in the Rockies, we wear a little bell when we go hiking to warn the bears that we're coming."

"A little bell? I'd have the fucking Liberty Bell tied to my ass. Clang! Clang! Here I come!"

We giggled softly at this absurd visual.

"Yeah, but add a tent and sleeping bags to what we're doing right now and we're not homeless, we're camping!"

"Give praise and thanks."

"What are you giving thanks for?" This wasn't a situation known to inspire gratitude. I have faith, but we're talking Biblical Job here.

"I came to this beach to die. Instead, it healed me. Jah must have other plans for me."

And like the aborigines of Australia who for millennium have buried themselves in the earth to heal, this homeless artist had found the same cure.

We lay in silence. I looked up at the full moon floating over the ocean. The sound of the waves gently lapping against the shore was soothing. It took a while for me to stop vibrating from the influx of humanity I had experienced in one day. Every person I met put me on high alert. You never knew what you were walking into, or how they would behave. At least in the business world, there was the façade of integrity. If someone was about to screw you, it was more subtle.

But the overall feeling I had was of intense excitement. There was no going back. I'd bought my ticket on this ride, and I was willing to take my chances. If homies were losing their mind out there, I thankfully couldn't hear them. The man lying nearby had found the one safe haven on this mad beach, under the stars, with only God to guide him. I decided to follow his lead. I couldn't explain why I was here. Maybe God had other plans for me, too.

3

IT NEVER RAINS IN CALIFORNIA

The heavy morning mist lay grey and damp on me like a soggy blanket. No wait, that was my blanket, and I was under it. I peered out of my nest at the pewter mist. This was California! Why was I so cold? I had spent the whole night awake, shivering. The cold sand, combined with the breeze off the ocean was more dampness than my Canadian anti-freeze could handle.

It was the kind of morning that would normally have kept me inside, writing, curled up by the fire, or at least in a comforter. Instead, I had the whole chilly day stretched out in front of me, outside. Then I thought of the homeless back in Calgary, Canada, who live on the streets when it is thirty degrees below zero Celsius. Time to cowboy up, Princess.

After what seemed like an eternity the sky began to lighten up and I heard movement under Rasta's blankets. I stared eagerly at the sand where he was buried, much the way my cat used to sit an inch away from me, waiting for me to open my eyes so I could feed him. Rasta peeked out and saw my goofy face.

"Morning, Camper!" I said brightly.

"Morning," he mumbled, "and I REFUSE to go camping."

In the distance I heard a loud diesel engine approaching. I started to get up but he hissed at me. “Rollers!” A police cruiser was on the boardwalk. I hid under my blanket. Once Rasta was sure we weren’t being watched he jumped out of his trench. “Let’s do it.”

He pulled out his shoes and bags, then heaved sand onto his blankets. I put my blanket in my bag, and filled in the trench. We sat with our backs to the Wall and watched a tractor pulling a rake chug by, grooming the sand for the day’s beach visitors. The tractor raked over the place where I had been buried moments before.

“Don’t catch many homies sleeping in around here, do you?”

“No live ones.”

“So, what do you guys do for showers?” I was ready to clean up for the day ahead.

He gave me a “you out of your mind?” look, then rummaged through his bags and produced a clean T-shirt. Pulling his arms into his sweater, he pulled the old T-shirt over his head. He carefully rolled the old one into a ball and put it in his ‘dirty clothes’ grocery bag. He pulled on the new one in the reverse order. It disappeared under the sweater.

“Well, can I at least take a dip in the ocean?”

“You see any homies get within ten feet of that water?”

Come to think of it, I hadn’t.

“Some sneak in during the night, but most are afraid of black water. During the day, lifeguards and rollers make sure only tourists hang out there.” He stared longingly at the nearby ocean that was so out of reach. “

"Can I buy you a coffee?" I asked.

"Bullion," came his reply. It was a term I would hear him use for anything that arrived unexpectedly as a treat. It was literally, 'worth its weight in gold', gold bullion; pirate's treasure.

We walked across the sand to the boardwalk. The overcast day had discouraged the tourists and Ocean Front Walk was deserted. Rasta led me to a small take out window. I smiled at the large cook who came to the window. His unshaven face glared back at me.

I wasn't used to that type of reception. My first job had been at the Calgary Stampede, a major tourist attraction and rodeo. I was taught to smile and say please and thank you to customers. It was part of giving great service.

Guess this guy hadn't gone to the same charm school and "Homeless" was now a huge neon sign on my forehead. No amount of smiling would thaw this guy. I placed my order. The Take Out Man disappeared and returned with two Styrofoam cups. I paid him and handed one to John. My twenty dollars was almost gone and this was only day three. I was going to have to find a way to eat for free soon.

"May I have some cream and sugar?" More smiling from me, more glaring and disgruntled noises from him. He tossed some packets of fake powdered milk and sugar at us.

"Thank you!"

The window slammed shut in my face. We retreated to a nearby bench.

An older man shuffled toward us. He nodded sadly at Rasta who gently touched him. "One Love, Brother".

"How are you, Rasta?" asked a tired voice.

"Dealin' with it."

Both men nodded gravely. The older man turned and looked at me. He gently touched my arm. I flinched but said good morning anyway. He nodded and moved on.

"It's okay, he's just making sure you're real," explained Rasta.

"Pardon?"

"Homie rule, if you can't touch it, don't talk to it. We all see too many ghosts on this beach to waste time talking to them."

Before long we were joined by David and Junior who had found other places to sleep away from the beach. They were good looking young men. I was sure that any number of women were willing to let them spend the night. Junior had his ever present copy of Kahlil Gibran's *The Prophet* open and was already scanning the boardwalk for female companionship. Rikki was nowhere in sight.

Another black Rastafarian bounded up the boardwalk toward us. His waist length dreadlocks were decorated like a Christmas tree - bobbles and tinsel everywhere. His skin had the blue black sheen of a crow. And his features were perfect. He was the African American counterpart of David. He was flamboyantly dressed in purple, giving him an effeminate air. Scarves were tied everywhere, including one around his head. He reminded me of Little Richard.

He came over to Rasta and they did a secret hand shake of sorts; knuckle wraps, finger snaps, and a shake. I was introduced.

"Poet, this is Canada. She's with the camp, now."

The Poet's eyebrows went up but he said nothing. I wondered if they were a couple. They were both artistic, and Rasta was definitely being a gentleman. He hadn't made a pass at me last night. In fact, he had made it very clear I was sleeping "over there".

While I pondered this, a leggy, once good looking California girl wandered over. She was wearing a string bikini top, shorts flying half way up her tanned butt and ankle bells. A dramatic scar zigzagged across her once pretty face. "Hey guys!"

"Hi Angel!" beamed Junior. Angel ignored him, gave me a sideways glance, and moved in on Rasta and the Poet.

"Hey, I'm just $100 short to pay for my studio time. Can you help me out with a twenty? My CD is almost finished."

The Poet and Rasta exchanged wary looks.

"Hey, I'm tapped out right now, Sweetie," apologized Rasta, "Maybe later if my crowns sell."

The Poet turned his back to her.

"Wow! You're recording a CD!" exclaimed Junior.

She flashed him a smile. "Loan me a twenty?"

"I'm broke," shrugged Junior apologetically.

Another man on the boardwalk caught her eye and she bounded away, hitching up her shorts so that even more cheek was winking at the tourists.

Rasta shook his head, "I been giving her twenties for months and she ain't shown me nothing 'cept those nasty pants."

"She isn't recording a CD?" Junior's faith in women did a hiccup.

"My daddy taught me the difference between bullshit and well chewed grass," grumbled the Poet.

"I heard that," agreed Rasta.

The Poet turned on his tiny radio cassette player and the sounds of Don Carlos reggae tune *Crazy Girl* began to play. Right on cue, a pretty blonde Lolita headed toward us, or more to the point, toward Junior. Her unnaturally outsized breasts were barely contained inside a tube top, and she had two large, angry women in tow.

The Poet swatted Junior on the head. "You better be getting your Gigolo ass over here."

Junior stood. "Hey, Penny."

She gazed adoringly at him; the two women behind her looked ready to eat him alive. "Mom, I'd like you to meet my boyfriend."

Rasta motioned to me and we all stood up and moved out of the way of the impending disaster. Junior silently mouthed the words "Help me!" as we departed.

A jogger wearing a *Sea Shepherd* T-shirt sprinted past us. Rasta recognized him and ran after him. "Hey, Sea Shepherd!" "Sea Shepherd" jogged backwards to see who was calling.

Rasta bounded up to him, dreadlocks flying. "Hey man, when do you want me to do some new T-shirts?"

The jogger smiled at him as they jogged in place together, the blond, tan, All-American next to the slender, bouncing black Dread. "Come by next week. We'll talk."

They waved and went their separate ways. Another homie business transaction completed.

We all settled down at another bench further along the boardwalk. An older black man slid onto the bench next to me. He had grey in his beard and a cataract was fogging up one eye.

He leaned close and touched my arm discreetly. "I heard you're a writer."

The beach tom-toms must have been hard at work last night. I nodded yes. Rasta moved quietly behind us and stood with the Poet and the rest of the camp, giving us some privacy. They pulled some rumpled cigarette butts out of their pockets, carefully chose the longest ones, and lit up.

The older man looked haunted and worn, but desperate to talk. "I'll give you something to write about."

His eyes darted around fueled by paranoia. He nodded toward my bag, so I got out a pad of paper and pencil. He spoke so fast, so desperately, I felt as if the FBI was just waiting around the corner to arrest him.

"I was a marine for twenty years. The military owns Canada. I seen them do things no one believes, illegal testing on people." He looked over his shoulder. I looked too, and saw my camp staring at us wide eyed. We turned back and huddled together conspiratorially.

He hurried on, "They put AIDS in the water, now

they're trying to cover their asses. Only gays were supposed to be their chemical dumping ground, they never planned on their own kids getting it."

He motioned over his shoulder to my camp, "See, they respect our privacy. It's illegal in this country for a black man to talk to a white woman. Only the Homies show respect. Everyone's using chemical warfare. General public doesn't even know we're at war. Marines were all experimented on: drugs, tests."

He paused, his eyes tearing up. He lifted his shirt and showed me his chest. A strange scar went the length of it. Not the kind of scar you get from heart surgery, but something different. Something rolled over in my stomach.

"Woke up one morning, they'd done this to me." His voice ended in a sob. He pulled his shirt back down. "Went to sleep in the barracks one night, woke up days later with this. No one told me what they'd done. They didn't explain nothin'."

This couldn't be true. Their motto was "To Serve and Protect". Why would a country's military want to harm its own men? Before I could ask him about it, he was off on another tangent.

"I see them at night, the space ships, don't you? When time's right, they're gonna come for me and take me away from here. Mine's been parked out there for years, just waiting." He gestured out toward the ocean, "I see it at night."

We sat for a moment. I had no response. Was he nuts? He didn't seem nuts, just desperate, and broken.

"Write any of it you want," he whispered to me, "People need to know the truth."

He nodded at Rasta and the boys, then got up and hurried away. I watched him disappear into a nearby alley, hunched over, scurrying like a beaten dog.

Rasta came back and sat down. “He ain’t said boo to nobody in two years.”

The group nodded their heads in agreement.

“Some of the things he said”, I had to stop and take a deep breath to slow my heart, “Sure, he left the planet a few times, but when he landed...” I shook my head, suddenly exhausted from the short, but brutal, confessional.

“I’m telling ya,” Rasta’s face was stone. “I’ve seen that same scar on a lot of black Marines living on the street.”

“And no one knows what happened?”

“You give up your personal rights when you join the military. I was in the Army for ‘Nam. They test all kinds of shit on the troops, especially black ones.”

He carefully gathered his bags and stood.

“What did he mean when he said the military owns Canada?” This part of the tirade had really caught my attention.

“When I worked for the L.A. Free Press a reporter found out your government allowed the U.S. military to test LSD on some university professors in Toronto during the 60s without telling them. They wanted to know if they could use it to gather intelligence. Your Canadian Professors thought they were going insane, some of them even committed suicide.”

And that's when something in my head exploded. "Wait! That's illegal! They can't do that to private citizens without..."

He held up his hand. "Now you're starting to feel some of the rage that put us on the street. Come on, time for the *Breakfast Club.*"

.

4

THE BREAKFAST CLUB

Our camp began its migration south to the famous *Breakfast Club*, the place where kind souls fed the homeless. We came abreast of Sonny Zorro, considered by all to be King of Venice Beach. He was an older Dread wearing a sparkly purple crown on his head. A car accident in high school had ended his football career and given him a slight limp. He was the first authentic vagabond I had ever met. He refused government assistance, and made his living as a part time musician-artist-free spirit; a true Hollywood hyphenate.

His life had become the stuff of legends. Some claim that Beatle John Lennon's famous "Lost Weekend" was spent with Sonny on Venice Beach. Others tell of Sonny finding a Picasso in a dumpster and giving it to his sister. He never wanted money, never wanted a life that revolved around it. He had been on the beach for seven years when I met him, and he would stay there until he died.

He nodded shyly at me when Rasta introduced us. He was pushing a shopping cart that was the most dazzling mobile work of art I had ever seen. It was known by all as "The Magic Bus". Every inch was decorated with colorful scarves, wind chimes and art. A brightly painted guitar rested in it.

A young, petite, dark haired woman in her twenties was with him. She gave Rasta the once over and showed off a new crown she was crocheting for

Sonny. Rasta's face grew hard as she flirted and possessively held Sonny's arm as they moved to the lineup for the *Breakfast Club.*

"Who's that?" I asked, meaning Sonny.

Rasta was focused on the woman. "She's a trip, that's who she is. I taught her to crochet, showed her how to hang on the beach. She's just down here to make her rich daddy mad. Hang with some black men until he caves in and gives her what she wants. She treats us like pets, not men."

The sudden flash of anger was so out of character I dropped the subject. But it was obvious he was watching me to see if I was made of the same stuff.

We arrived at Windward Plaza, a huge circular concert pavilion next to the Basketball Courts and Muscle Beach. This was where the Breakfast Club took place every weekday morning. Blown out drunks and crack addicts stood in line with mothers and children. Many were dressed for work. The high price of housing and rentals kept this workforce curbed. We got in line with the rest of the beach residents.

I was impressed with the civility of it all. "Everyone sure is well behaved."

"We're down," said the Poet, "but we're not out."

A weary looking Jesus impersonator went by dragging a cross. His crown of thorns was plastic, and his robe was a white bed sheet. Pink flip flops completed the ensemble. Rasta gave him the "One Love" sign. The Venice Beach Jesus nodded back.

We passed an Asian man standing at the chain link fence with a chalk board. Nicknamed "The Prophet', he too was dressed in white sheets tied at the waist like a Franciscan Monk. His long beard was braided; his black hair reached his waist.

The message on his chalk board read, *"Be not forgetful to entertain strangers, for thereby some have entertained angels unawares. – Hebrew 13:2"*

Rasta again held up his index finger, "One love, Brother".

The self-proclaimed prophet did the same. We shuffled along. The folding tables the St. Joseph's volunteers had set up at the entrance to the pavilion were almost within reach.

Junior caught up with us, subdued after his confrontation with the angry women.

Rasta shook his head. "I keep telling you; don't mess with that little girl. You're homeless! Your emotions aren't under control. Besides, you're putting your brothers at risk!"

Junior sulked and shuffled along in line with the rest of us. We signed in and were each handed a brown bag and container of orange juice. We all smiled and said thank you. In front of us was a sea of round concrete tables painted like clocks. Ironic feeding the homeless here; people who had lost all track of time were eating off clocks.

We found a spot and sat on the half moon benches. Our table filled up quickly. Many homies swung by just to check in with Rasta and exchange some news. An older man joined us and sat down with a box full of books strapped to a collapsible dolly. His nickname was "Happy" and he appeared to be just that. He had beautiful long, wavy white hair and a neatly trimmed beard. He nodded at me and placed R.D. Laing's book, *The Divided Self: An Existential Study in Sanity and Madness* on the table. He appeared to be a university professor on sabbatical, complete with a sweater vest.

We all opened up our brown bags and took out the neatly wrapped processed cheese on white sandwiches, fresh oranges, and week old pastries. Everyone silently compared pastries and the trading began; the cracked Bear's Claw for the Cinnamon Twist, a sugar donut for one with sprinkles. The Poet scored big with a chocolate covered Boston cream. He held it close and shook his head, no trades on this one.

I bit into my sandwich with glee. Normally I was all granola and organic, but today I couldn't wolf down my processed cheese treasure fast enough.

"Where's Rikki?" I asked, scanning the crowd.

"That Schizo?" chimed in David.

"Crazy child," was the Poet retort.

"*Mystics swim in seas where Schizophrenics drown,*" quoted Happy.

"Fuck that, he's a pain in the ass!" said the Poet.

"Hey, Happy," said Junior, "how come animals aren't Schizophrenic?"

"They might be," mused Happy, stroking his beard, "We just haven't found one willing to tell us its delusions."

"I heard that," said Rasta.

I stared at the sugar coated donut in my hand and remembered something we studied in microbiology when I was getting my degree. "Linus Pauling says sugar makes you crazy."

We all looked at the bombs of destruction in our sticky hands, and gleefully wolfed them down.

Seeing the washrooms were unlocked, I excused myself and made a beeline for them. There wasn't the urgency this morning that I thought there would be, probably because I was so dehydrated. It was the kind of washroom I would expect a prison to have; no doors on the stalls, the mirror was a large square piece of reflective, unbreakable metal. I hurried to the farthest stall, hoping no one would stumble on me, and hovered over the toilet bowl like a flying saucer.

When I returned to our "clock", Rasta was watching a nearby woman out of the corner of his eye. His gaze flickered between her and David. She was in her early twenties and was doing an impromptu belly dance. She was dressed early flower child in a tie-dyed floor length skirt with bells on her ankles. David spotted her and started tearing his sandwich into tiny little pieces.

The Poet realized we had a ticking time bomb in our midst. "Oh, shit."

The dancer looked at David then danced her way over to a nearby weight-lifter. She wrapped herself around him. The man reached over, squeezed her breast...and we had lift off.

David leapt up from the table. "You lousy, stinking whore!"

"Here we go." Rasta slowly put away his breakfast and prepared for the worst. Several nearby homies began to jeer at David, egging him on.

"Hey, man! Shut the fuck up!"

"Wha'sa matter? You pussy whipped?"

The dancer and weight-lifter moved away. David spun around in frustration, looking for something to take his anger out on. Then he saw it: the pay phone. Screaming he rushed over and began kicking and shaking it. The jeering and hooting from the Breakfast Club got louder. He finally ripped it off the wall. Money jingled to the pavement, a Homie Gold Rush. Everyone scrambled to pick up the change.

Rasta grabbed David, moving him back to our table just as two undercover cops came out of the nearby washroom. "Chill, homeboy, they just be waiting to kick your ass."

David sank back down on the bench, staring despondently at the table. The two cops tried to break up the crowd scrambling for change.

"Who are they?" I asked.

"Undercover cops," hissed Junior.

That, for some reason, gave me the giggles. They looked so out of place, I don't know how they could think they were incognito. Their hair was ruthlessly short. They were dressed in golf shirts and pastel colored pants. I had yet to see a homie dressed like that. I obviously hadn't run into the homeless golfers yet.

"Hey Poet," said Rasta, "aren't those the two who hustled you yesterday?"

"Those gay bashers? Sure are. They hustled ME, then tried to ticket me!"

"They ought a quit." Rasta flicked his fingers in a snapping gesture.

Happy was ready with another quote, "*If we are unaware of how mad we are, we are even less aware of how mad we need to be. Madness may be a natural healing process of the mind."*

"Well, this boy be breaking down for real, an all over some trashy game player," admonished Rasta.

David retreated into a shell, head sunk even further down.

"There's some real tacky hussies out here, real fruit loops. You find a good one, you better hang on." Rasta tried to sooth David's frayed nerves.

"Amen," chirped Junior.

"Shut up!" spat the Poet in true Little Richard form.

I sat, watching the mini drama before me, and tried to remember the last time I had witnessed anything this "real" in my world; probably never. Everyone was so good at stifling their thoughts and emotions, being politically correct, saying what was expected. I honestly couldn't remember witnessing such an honest exchange.

I leaned over to Happy. "What's this book about?"

Happy smiled, always ready for a scholarly chat. He spoke to me quietly so David couldn't hear. "Laing believed that madness is a result of individuals being put in impossible situations, where they are unable to conform to the conflicting expectations of their peers, leading to a 'lose-lose situation' and immense mental distress for the individuals concerned. Bateson articulated a related theory of schizophrenia as stemming from double bind situations. Madness was therefore an expression of this distress."

"When the person who was supposed to be David's parent and protector at home had instead harmed him, he experienced madness. He's very close to taking the path that Rikki has chosen."

I looked over at David. If he became schizophrenic, in this society, it would be the end of him.

Happy continued. "On the positive side, Laing felt madness could be a transformative episode whereby the process of undergoing mental distress was compared to a shamanic journey. The traveler could return from the journey with important insights, and may even have become a wiser and more grounded person as a result."

These words would haunt me for years. When I experienced my own descent into homelessness and despair, the wisdom of this camp often helped me cope.

A cute teenager seemed to be working her way toward our table. She was slender with shoulder length sun bleached hair, Capri pants, and a tank top. Once she got closer, however, I realized she was actually older than me. The deep lines in her tanned face reflected a hard life. "Wash Day!" she announced.

The men immediately dug into their bags and started handing over dirty laundry and spare change. Rasta pulled out the t-shirts he had carefully rolled into balls and stored in grocery bags. He handed them over with a fistful of change. She hung each bag from a separate hook in her shopping cart, making sure the laundry didn't get mixed up. This woman had obviously been someone's mother. And sure enough, her nickname was "Mom".

"You hear about the assassin?" she whispered.

We all moved in closer to hear this homie news.

"They say the famous assassin known as 'Carlos' is hiding out here on the beach."

We all looked around as if the master of disguise would actually be sitting nearby with a name tag on. His reputation had reached mythic proportions, with every terrorist activity in the world being somehow tied to him.

"I thought he only operated in Europe. Why would he be here?" I asked the gathered think tank.

"Perfect place to hide; no one here has an identity," replied Happy. "They look at us as a mob, not as people."

"Isn't he the most wanted man alive?" Junior asked.

Mom nodded, obviously on a mini 'high' from the intrigue of it all.

"Now don't you go lookin' for him." Rasta touched her arm. She gave him a wide eyed innocent stare. Rasta grinned at her and changed the subject, "Hey, Sweetie, when are you going to introduce us to those wild children of yours?"

The camp burst out laughing.

"You think your camp can handle them?"

"Now you be hallucinating for real!" Rasta laughed.

Everyone began to pack up their things. Rasta went to the St. Joseph's tables and the volunteers handed him the last of the bagged lunches.

"What makes you so special?" I asked.

"They know I'll hand them out to anyone who missed Breakfast Club. Hey, Junior, go find Rikki for me."

Junior waved him off. He was in hot pursuit of a cute girl on roller blades and already had his copy of *The Prophet* out.

Rasta spun around to the Poet. “Come on, man, I got art to do, go find Rikki.”

“A person can grow old lookin’ for Rikki, I’m busy.”

We moved down the boardwalk and the camp set up under an open slat pagoda. It didn’t offer any respite from the rain, but the illusion of a roof seemed to satisfy the group.

Happy put out his books on the picnic bench and covered them in plastic. Before long homies were browsing the books. A mere dime could buy you a book for the day. Without addresses, the homeless couldn’t get library cards, so Happy became their library. I peered at the eclectic selection of books; everything from Harlequin romances to books on philosophy were available. I nodded and smiled at Happy. He tipped his invisible hat to me, and took care of his next customer.

5

RUNNINS

Rasta and I set off to find Rikki. We had barely walked ten paces down the boardwalk when Rasta's face suddenly went hard. Two police on foot moved in close and confronted him. "Let's see some ID."

"What did I do?"

The police moved in closer, "Just show us some ID."

Rasta reached into his pocket and one of the cops unclipped his gun. Rasta gave him a look. "You wanna shoot? Or you wanna see some ID?"

The cop removed his hand from his gun and crossed his arms.

"Don't you want to see my ID?" I demanded.

They wouldn't even look at me, just kept staring at Rasta. I couldn't believe someone could be stopped on the street in this day and age and have to produce papers. Wasn't that the deal in Nazi Germany?

Rasta pulled out a worn, brown leather wallet. It was bulging with everything that was important to him in the world. Slowly, thoughtfully, he began extricating old photos, papers, and memorabilia. He carefully unfolded each piece of paper, read it, then moved on to the next. My rage started to dissipate as I realized what he was doing; he was going to make them earn the right to see his identification papers. The police fidgeted impatiently. Finally, an old, faded ID card was produced. Each policeman took a glance, and then nodded to him.

"Thank you, Mr. Scott. A woman was robbed near here; suspect's a dread, name Enriquez. "

Rasta nodded and they moved on.

"Why didn't they ask me for my ID?"

"Cuz you got an international visa for a face: blonde woman with blue eyes."

I reached for his ID as he was about to put it away. "Can I see that?"

He handed over the ancient piece of identification. It was his U.S. Army projectionist license. Only the huge, compassionate eyes looked familiar to me as I gazed at the youthful, short haired man in the picture: John Scott. Finally, I had a name.

"I was the Army projectionist, used to show movies in the barracks."

Somehow a dreadlocked artist didn't fit my image of GI Joe. "So, you were drafted?"

"Nope, volunteered for Vietnam, can you believe that?" Rasta shook his head at his own stupidity. "I thought it would make the old man like me."

"Did it?"

He shook his head "No".

"I heard boot camp's a killer."

"Weren't nothing compared to my Old Man. He was military to the bone, made Boot Camp look like Disney World."

We ducked into a back alley and began our search for Rikki. There was no telling where the voices had led the Schizophrenic youth, so every nook and cranny had to be checked. It was like looking for a lost kitten. Lifting up the lid of a particularly nasty dumpster, I couldn't believe the homeless really slept in these. They smelt like pig farms; the same acrid, sour, vomit inducing aroma. I was grateful we were sleeping in the earth.

We did a zigzag search pattern; one block in the alley, one block on Ocean Front Walk. I hoped we would find him before another finger joint was sacrificed. Finally, we spotted him in the distance. He was standing on the boardwalk facing a three storey walk up apartment. Huge windows faced the ocean; a large set of double doors sat at the top of six concrete stairs. The effect was that of a giant Jack O' Lantern sitting on the sidewalk. And Rikki was talking to it, or rather, mumbling at it. I hung back and let the homie therapist I was with do his thing.

"Hey, Homeboy." Rasta John gently approached the teenager. Rikki mumbled, eyes down, unaware of the man standing next to him. Rasta shook his head, "We got too many people in this here conversation. Hey! Rikki!"

Rikki looked up, surfacing for a brief moment in time, before plunging back into the depths of his psychosis. Rasta reached out and touched him. It was the lightest of touches, like a feather, but to someone whose nerves were all exposed and raw on the surface of his being, it was like an electric shock. Rikki was jolted back to awareness. He looked up mournfully. "Know what they told me to do?"

"Who, Homeboy?"

"Them," said Rikki, sweeping his arms in a large circle, indicating the crowd assembled around him.

Rasta shook his head. "Only thing I see around here is your raggedy butt."

Rikki became more agitated, "They said I can't go to the Breakfast Club until I jump off this building."

We all stared up at the top of the building. Maybe an agile cat could survive a three storey fall, but Rikki definitely had more mass and less floating power.

Rasta stroked the stubble on his chin. "Well, if it was me, I'd try something smaller first, like those stairs over there." We all looked at the six steps leading to the front door. "If that worked, then I'd try the bigger stuff."

Rikki mumbled and fidgeted, eyes darting to the stairs, the roof, the man beside him, the crowd arguing with him. What worlds were spinning through his head? Who was talking to him? Memories flooded back on me, memories I worked hard to forget; lying in bed as a child, trying not to breathe loudly, lying bone straight so my hands wouldn't touch the edge of the bed. My bed was surrounded by hooded figures. I was afraid that if any part of me ventured to the edge of the bed I'd be pulled off and disappear. I'd lie like that all night. If I started to drift off to sleep someone would yell my name, jolting me awake.

My parents tried to pay me to stay in my room, but I never made a dime. My brother let me keep a sleeping bag in his room so I could sleep on the floor. I thought I was insane, but I managed to get through the days alright, even became an honor student. Until night fell and the ordeal began again.

As an adult I often wondered if I was Schizophrenic. But then I learned to meditate and finally gained control of my mind. I made a deal with the universe, if it wanted to talk to me, just deliver it as a bright idea, or a soft voice in my head - no visions, no noises. So far, it was working.

Years later, when my own son was seven, I asked him if he saw things in his room at night. He nodded timidly. “Faces come out of the wall and talk to me.”

“Are they friendly or do they scare you?”

“They scare me.”

“Then tell them to leave.”

I wondered if every child on Earth went through this without guidance. I told him he was allowed to tell them to leave, it was a universal law. Free will and all that. A week later I asked him if he still saw faces at night. He said they came the next night, he told them to leave, and they left. Problem solved.

Unfortunately Rikki had never been armed with this information, and now these visions ruled his reality. He stood on the boardwalk, listening to the debates raging in his head. We waited.

Rasta John gently repeated his advice, “If it was me, I’d try something smaller first, like those stairs over there, if that worked, then I’d try the bigger stuff.”

Rikki finally nodded, “They say this is sound advice.”

“Oh, they do, do they?” Rasta wiped the sweat from his forehead as Rikki marched up the stairs and on to the concrete balustrade. He spread his arms wide. A look of peace spread across his face. He closed his eyes. The sun broke through the clouds and shone on him. He looked like an angel. Then he jumped.

For a split second he was suspended, floating high above us. Then he plummeted to earth like a rock. He hit the pavement hard tearing his jeans. He put his hands out to stop the skin ripping skid he was in but his momentum kept him going. His hands tore open, embedded with gravel and dirt. He came to rest with his face planted on the sidewalk. We rushed to his side.

Rasta knelt down and gently lifted him up. "What did they say?"

"Nothin."

"Hello."

Tears streamed down Rikki's child like face. We helped him back to the pagoda where the camp was attempting to get some relief from the rain. Rikki sat on a bench and everyone quickly went to work cleaning the gravel out of his knees and hands. Rasta pulled out one of the bag lunches.

"Hey, Homeboy, we saved you some breakfast."

Rikki took it gratefully and began eating. The wind blew a large black garbage bag toward us. Rasta snared it, opened it up and climbed in. Rikki watched the bag, mesmerized. Then Rasta's beaming face peeked out, "John Doe's Condo!"

Rikki laughed gleefully, which made us all laugh. We were back on track. Our laughter attracted two new visitors to the beach. Cuba and N.Y. made their way over to our table.

"Mind if we join you?" asked N.Y., a tall, good looking black man in his thirties with well kept dreads. He was dressed in an expensive track suit and the Adidas on his feet were worth more than this entire camp made in a year. “We heard this is the place to be on Venice.”

“I heard that,” said Rasta, “One love, brother.” He shook hands with the young man.

“I’m from New York, just here on vacation.”

“An’ you came all that way to hang with some homies? You ought a quit.”

The rest of us were staring at his companion Cuba in disbelief. He was wearing a thousand dollar handmade suit and carrying matching luggage.

The Poet gave him the once over, “The Bell Captain has stepped out but I’m sure someone here would be happy to relieve you of your luggage.”

The group snickered.

“I just got off the plane from Cuba,” said Cuba.

“You don’t say.”

N.Y. interjected, “We met at the airport, and I convinced him this was the place to be.”

“Hello.”

Finally, blessedly, the rain stopped and the sun broke through the clouds.

“You look like you play basketball,” Rasta challenged N.Y.

“Hell yeah!”

“Come on.” Rasta took off down the boardwalk. And like good campers, we all followed.

*****

An hour later we were on the court, a basketball game in full swing. The Venice Beach basketball courts are the true testing ground for anyone thinking they can play. On weekends some of the best players in the world show up for good old fashioned street games: no referees, no pay, just fresh air one hundred yards from the ocean. A group of ragamuffins like us wouldn't be allowed near this Mecca on the weekend. But midweek on a cloudy day it was all ours.

The court was wedged in between Windward Plaza, where we enjoyed breakfast, and Muscle Beach, where women enjoyed pseudo-naked men pumping iron in "The Pit". Arnold Schwarzenegger's days of pumping iron here were long since gone, but those eager to follow in his footsteps were grunting, strutting, and performing, while observers lined the fence, taking in every lift, pull and jerk. Quite frankly, I preferred the *Fat Albert* collection of souls I was with on the basketball court.

I played basketball in high school. My brother had played at the Olympic level. Scanning the players on the court, I had to admit this was the most eclectic, bizarre team I'd ever joined.

Rasta John, with his small stature and slender build, would never have survived a legitimate game. But his unique blend of child-like enthusiasm, cheerleading skills, and heckling ability made him an MVP. He was blissfully unaware of his own limitations. Anyone getting their hands on the ball had to deal with his bounding, hollering intimidation. Nine times out of ten he could steal the ball and pass it to a shooter.

Homies and drummers sat in the bleachers, enjoying the show. The drummers pounded out applause for each basket. Cuba's snake skin suitcases, or whatever dead animal they were made from, sat courtside along with his expensive shoes, socks, and jacket.

N.Y. was by far the best player, but I was making some pretty impressive shots if I do say so myself. After accidentally grabbing some passing family jewels, and delivering some unfortunate kicks to the groin, I had proven myself dangerous and the men gave me a wide berth, allowing me to pull off some not bad long shots. I avoided going under the basket for rebounds because frankly there were too many "balls" under there already, a girl could get in trouble.

Our team had just scored and was basking in the cheers when Rasta John suddenly grabbed my arm and hustled me off the court.

"What?" I looked around in confusion.

"Rollers."

All I could see were two badly dressed couples I presumed were tourists. Their Bermuda shorts, Hawaiian shirts and straw hats had "Cruise Line" written all over them. Then they made their move. They walked boldly onto the court and surrounded N.Y.

N.Y. smiled at them. "Want to play?" He held out the ball to one of the men and was immediately handcuffed.

Cuba faded into the crowd and vanished.

"What the hell? I know my rights! You can't do this!" yelled N.Y.

I spun on Rasta. "How can they do that? They didn't read him his rights!"

"They can haul his black ass anywhere they want. You be forgetting you grew up in Disneyland."

The tension on the bleachers was primal, a riot waiting to happen. This search for the elusive dreadlocked man named "Enriquez" was wearing down the homies. Rasta watched the police interrogation of N.Y until he decided enough was enough.

He stood up on the top bleacher and started heckling, "Oh, Enriquez! Yoo hoo! Enriquez!"

The rest of the homies quickly picked it up and began waving and hollering at the undercover cops. "Enriquez! Where are you? Enriquez!"

The cops glared at us and moved N.Y. to a police cruiser. They frisked him and took out his wallet from his shorts. N.Y. stood rigid, indignant, ready to erupt. Finally, the police unlocked the handcuffs and let him go. He grabbed his wallet and stormed back to the bleachers. He began throwing things around, venting his frustration. Rasta moved in on him. "Chill, Homeboy. You never been cuffed before?"

"Hell, No! I work for the press in New York. I have never been treated like...like..."

"Like you was black?" asked Rasta innocently.

Nearby homies fell out laughing.

Rasta spoke to him soothingly, in a low voice. "You ain't never been curbed, Homeboy. Don't get yourself so upset you fly off the handle, cuz that's what they're waiting for. You're putting us all in jeopardy. You got to maintain some control."

I realized I was late for my morning check in with

my roommate and made a beeline for the pay phone courtside. My coins jingled into the box as I watched my camp. I couldn't help but smile. People were sharing food, information, advice, and gradually calming N.Y. down.

My roommate, still living in my alternative reality, picked up on the first ring. "Where the hell have you been? It's almost noon, I was ready to call the cops!" She shrieked in that hysterical, yet touchingly protective manner of hers.

"You don't have to worry about cops, they're everywhere down here." It took me several minutes to make her realize I was fine. In fact, I was enjoying myself. When I decided to live on the street, I didn't think I would be feeling so elated, so alive, so free.

"You're playing basketball?" she asked, incredulous.

"Yeah, we're winning!" Deadly silence sat on the other end of the line. "Hello?"

"What if your family calls? What am I supposed to tell everyone?"

"Nothing, you don't have to tell anyone anything. This is my life."

It wasn't what she wanted to hear. Her home was full of New Age books telling her to create her own reality, but she didn't really believe it. She was convinced she needed to fight and claw her way up the corporate ladder, pay a mortgage too high for her income, and keep up appearances. And I was NOT supposed to be having fun!

She hung up in disgust. I put the phone back and wondered what the hell was going on. A slow realization crept up on me. I was at peace, and that was pissing her off. I had taken the first tentative steps; stepping away from the brainwashing society places on us and amazingly my head hadn't exploded.

What were we all conditioned to be so afraid of? Was there a game master in the sky spying on me who might realize I was a flawed game piece and have me replaced? I had thrown down the gauntlet to the Universe, and it was showing me true lightness of being. I was being me, maybe for the first time in my life, and I wasn't ready to give that up.

I walked back to the court and saw Rasta watching me intently. "I've got to get some cash from that knucklehead to do his artwork. Wanna come?"

"Runnins?" I grinned. "Sure."

*****

Once again, we were standing outside the Jamaican's metal door in the alley.

"Go away," the perpetually high parrot squawked.

"I can't believe he stood me up again!" Rasta John shook his head wearily, the possibility of a day's work, and a day's pay, evaporating in front of him.

"How much money do you need for art supplies?"

"Couple hundred dollars if this was legit. I'll be happy to see ten bucks from this knucklehead."

We wandered away, John deep in thought.

6

HOMIE ART STUDIO

Once back on the boardwalk, John spotted a solution to his artistic dilemma. He wandered over to a man and they talked quietly. Soon two baggies of marijuana changed hands.

We moved further on and once again John wandered away from me to some surfers on the beach. They bought the bags and John pocketed the cash. I've never been one to condone drug deals, but I had worked in the advertising industry for years back in Canada, and loved watching the artists and creative directors do their thing. I was curious to see if this homie was the real deal, and if he could pull off color separations for a printer working on the street.

He came back to me. "We're flush, let's roll."

He was off like a shot. I had to hustle to keep up with him. We left Ocean Front Walk and headed inland on South Venice Boulevard. Traffic was heavy, and no one else was walking. We had entered the world of the non-homies; people in cars.

After three days on the beach, it was jarring being around the exhaust and the pace again. Not that I preferred the unique fragrance of urine on Venice Beach, but I had actually stopped noticing it. We walked for several miles until we came to an art supply store. We walked in and John gave the One Love sign to the store owner. The man nodded and left us alone. He knew this artist.

John stood in the middle of an aisle, a look of pure bliss on his face. This was his world, or had been. He reverently touched the tubes of oil paints, the brushes, and canvases. Paintings filled the walls.

“Are you a painter?”

He nodded and checked out a large stretched canvas. “I worked in a gallery on 5th Avenue in New York. I was bad; worked in the store during the day, painted at night.”

He picked out some black markers of varying thicknesses, a roll of tracing paper, white out, masking tape, and a bright white square of cardboard. He took it to the cash register and carefully counted out the money. With his bag of supplies and change in hand, we were on the move again. He set off at a brisk pace, then noticed I was lagging behind.

“You okay?”

“Sorry, I’m tired. Now I know what you meant about taking care of your feet.”

“I heard that. You can sit when we get to the copy shop.”

We moved along North Venice Boulevard and onto Pacific. For all the exotic street names, I was disappointed at the blandness of the real deal. This concrete jungle was brutally bare. The houses had cement for lawns. The city didn’t bother planting anything on the boulevards or sidewalks with all the gang related violence going on. It was just an expanse of dusty roads strewn with litter choked exhausted palm trees.

“Can I ask you something?” I had been waiting for the right time to ask this question.

"Sure."

"How did you end up on the street?"

He paused. I knew it was a big step, letting me in, past the brave mask, past the image he had so carefully constructed over a fractured soul.

"I was tired of selling my paintings in galleries where they take the framing cost off the top, then their commission, then hand me a couple of dollars. I couldn't hang. I rented a warehouse and turned it into an artist co-op. Covered the walls in newspapers, let other artists put up their work along with mine. We had huge group shows. Money went straight to the artist, and they'd kick me back a little something to cover rent. I lived in the back behind a curtain. Everything was going great. Then, one day, the real landlord showed up."

"Real Landlord?"

"Turns out my 'landlord' was actually renting the place. Pocketed my cash and never paid the rent. The real landlord never saw a dime and threw me out."

He stopped walking and tried to wipe the pain from his eyes. "I remember walking out the door, going to the corner. I looked left, then right, then left again. Realized I had nowhere to go. Sat down on the curb. That's where Sonny found me. He brought me to the beach."

There it was, the story I'd been waiting to hear. All the places I'd rented, the great landlords who cleaned rugs and painted walls and appreciated my presence. I'd never heard of this kind of corruption. But like he said, I grew up in Disneyland. We walked on in silence for a time; then he figured he might as well let me hear it all.

"The night you arrived on the beach, up at the Santa Monica camp, you know what I was doing?"

"No."

"I was getting ready to set myself on fire. During the Vietnam War a Buddhist Monk set himself on fire to protest the war. I've been on this beach for two years, and nothing has changed. Nobody cares about us; we're the lepers of society. I figured my death might have more impact than my life."

"No, it wouldn't." I took his hand and held it. For once, he didn't flinch. He let the small comfort being offered sink in.

"Last summer, the Pope came to L.A. They didn't want him to see us living on the street. They rounded us up, put us on buses, and drove us out of town. It took us a week to walk back, but we did. It's a trip."

We walked on in silence. I remembered seeing some of the Pope's speech on T.V. from the comfort of my penthouse in Canada.

The Pope admonished the United States, "*Is present day America becoming less sensitive, less caring toward the poor, the weak, the stranger, the needy? It must not.*"

*****

We arrived at a little self service copy centre and walked in. The young tattooed, pierced, purple-haired girl behind the counter smiled at John. Everyone working there looked like they played in a punk band at night, and they obviously appreciated John's eccentric look. For once, I was the weird one in a sea of artistic souls.

“Hey Rasta,” beamed one of the girls. “How you been?”

“Dealin’ with it,” he replied with that flying snap of his fingers. “Can we borrow a stool?

A stool was retrieved from behind the counter and I gratefully collapsed onto it. Rasta John set up at one of the copiers and pulled out the tattered concert poster of the Jamaican. First, he photocopied the poster on a light setting. He took the copy and used the *White Out* to remove unnecessary marks. He held the paper as far away from him as he could.

“I need longer arms.” Obviously, some reading glasses were in order, but he carried on. He darkened the Jamaican’s portrait with the markers then made a copy of the new piece. It came out as a beautiful line drawing. Several of the clerks had wandered over to watch and nodded appreciatively at each incarnation of the poster. I was impressed. Rasta gave me a wink and paid for the copies.

As we made our way back to the camp I found we were walking in unison, bags bumping against our bodies in rhythm. It had become a walking meditation, these runnins. There was peace in not being able to accomplish everything at light speed zipping through traffic. The short break at the copy shop had given me my second wind, and I was able to keep up with this deceptively fit dread.

We were crossing the street when something flashed at him from the gutter. He wandered over and fished through the debris. Smiling, he stood up holding a pair of glasses. He cleaned them off, put them on, and pulled a book out of his bag. He grinned.

“You’re not going to tell me they’re the right prescription.”

"Give praise and thanks," he murmured as he carefully put them away in his bag.

"I grew up playing by a whole bunch of rules that don't seem to exist here."

"I played by the rules, too."

*****

As we neared the boardwalk we passed a construction site. Wood remnants filled a nearby dumpster. Rasta John hurried over to it.

He hollered at the construction workers up on the second storey rigging. "Hey, Man, okay if I help myself?"

They waved an okay to him and he carefully picked through the two by fours and plywood sheets until he found what he was looking for; a section of half inch plywood, about eighteen inches square. He held it up proudly.

"Welcome to my art studio!"

*****

The rain stuttered on and off all morning, then remembered this was California and quit altogether. Mom, our laundry lady and Rikki were at the Laundromat doing the camp's laundry and keeping dry. Junior had gone to clean graffiti off a local storefront. Happy was busy renting books, and Rasta was hard at work on the cover art. David hadn't appeared, but I hoped he'd found somewhere warm and dry to nest for the day.

This camp was unique from the others on the beach in that everyone found ways to make money. No one was allowed to beg; it was a camp rule. I hadn't come up with a homie occupation yet, so I read Bob

Marley's biography *Catch a Fire,* with the hopes it would shed some light on the Rastafarian culture I had landed in.

The inspiration for the movement was Haile Selassie I, the former Emperor of Ethiopia. Rastafarians consider him to be God incarnate and the messiah promised in the Bible. Ethiopia is one of the oldest nations in the world, and considered by many to be the birthplace of mankind. Haile Selassie I ruled Ethiopia from 1930 to 1974. The name *Rastafari* comes from Haile Selassie I's original name.

He was never a Rastafarian himself, but was a member of the Ethiopian Orthodox Church. However, he believed in tolerance for all religions.

"*Nobody can interfere in the realm of God, therefore we should tolerate and live side by side with those of other faiths, we wish to recall here the spirit of tolerance shown by our Lord Jesus Christ.*"

Rastafarians are encouraged not to drink or do drugs, to eat only natural, healthy (Ital) foods, and read the Bible a chapter a day. The smoking of herb (marijuana) is considered a sacrament, and, as Rasta John had so succinctly explained, it keeps them from putting a brick through someone's window. From what I had seen on the beach, it was a religion for angry black men; a religion stripped down to its simplest forms, with guidelines on how to live, and to rise above the state a person is born into. It was a religion for poor oppressed people and California surfers.

The Rastafarians stress loyalty to their vision of "Zion", and rejection of modern society, "Babylon", which they see as thoroughly corrupt. I would hear the two terms daily on my stay at the beach. Philosophical conversations about the collapse of "Babylon" would rage far into the night.

Rasta had been on the receiving end of so much racism, he said had seen the belly of the beast. "This country is rotting from within. It doesn't take care of its people."

I remembered my father reading about the collapse of the Roman and Nazi empires and telling me that both failed because they stopped looking after their home base and expanded too far into other countries. They were so far a field that people at home were starving and going without basic necessities. Was this going to be America's fate as well?

Bob Marley was also considered to be a prophet, and his peaceful Reggae music was credited with calming the riots in the ghettos of Jamaica. Here, on Venice Beach, it was calming the homies. John had a small cassette player on the batik cloth between us.

The sounds of Bob Marley's song "*Exodus*" filled the air, "*We know where we're going, and we know where we're from. We live in Babylon, we're going to our father's land.*"

I closed the book and watched the Rastafarian artist in front of me. Did he dream of Zion? Of one day leaving Babylon, in this case Los Angeles, in search of Paradise? Given what the homeless black vets on this beach had suffered at the hands of the U.S. government, I could understand their dream of Zion.

The dreadlocks worn by some Rastafarians are symbolic of the journey the slaves made from Africa. They spent months chained up in ships and couldn't groom or keep their hair short, so it knotted into dreadlocks. Now, dreadlocks were symbolic of that journey, and of the Rastafarian Lion. I had to admit, looking at John's hair, it resembled a proud lion's mane. John told me the first time he grew dreads he realized they were "vanity dreads", based on ego and attracting women, so he cut them off. This second time around he wanted to have them for spiritual reasons.

The cover art he was working on was coming along at an amazing pace. John had taped the oversize photocopy of the Jamaican's portrait onto the white cardboard, then taped that onto the plywood, then three layers of tracing paper over that. Each layer of tracing paper was for each of the three primary colors, red, yellow, and blue. The printer would use these overlays to create the spectrum of all colors.

Sections he wanted to appear blue were on the blue tracing paper, same with yellow and red. Anything that was to be green had to be drawn and matched identically on the yellow page and blue pages. They would combine at the printers to produce green.

All colors created from mixing the primary colors had to be identical on the appropriate pages. These days computers do this, and ad agencies charge hundreds, if not thousands of dollars for full color separations. This guy was doing it for twenty bucks on a piece of plywood. I watched his hands holding the felt markers with a lightness of touch that hinted at decades of practice.

He held the pens sideways, all fingers touching the shaft, unlike writers who hold pens upright in a tight grip. His strokes glided across the page in a beautiful abstract design. He practiced doing letters for awhile on some scrap paper, then, a new font created, began to place it on the page as well.

"You should sell that to *Letraset*," I suggested.

"You know how to do that?"

"I was in advertising; it's easy enough to find out."

He smiled to himself and kept working. Junior and David came running up, eager to share their day's journey. "I found some yarn for your crowns," beamed David.

He handed over a mass of colored yarn, tangled up in grass. Rasta thanked him as if it was the Crown Jewels.

David couldn't wait to blurt out his news. "I met a guy said I could stay at his house, FREE!"

"No strings?" John was cynical.

"No strings!"

"Who is this guy?"

"You've seen him; he has that expensive condo down by the pier."

"White hair, always wearing pastels?"

"Yeah! That's the guy." David was beside himself, a chance to get off the beach.

"He's gay. There are strings attached, you'd be, like, his marionette." Rasta imitated a marionette, sending Junior into fits of laughter. David's face fell.

"So, I shouldn't go live with him?"

"You gay?"

David shook his head, end of discussion. Suddenly the group turned as one and faced the board walk. Their internal homie clocks indicated a scheduled event was about to happen.

It was the guy with the braided beard, the one who had scared the crap out of me my first morning in Venice. He was hunkered down on some steps leading to the boardwalk. He saw us all watching and put his finger to his lips for silence. He peered around the concrete wall and judged the distance of some approaching tourists. Nothing like a drug-fueled Leprechaun, all dressed in green, to make your visit to Venice Beach perfect.

As the tourists came abreast of him he went into action. Screaming, he rolled down the steps and fell, spread eagled, in front of them. The women screamed; the men jumped out of their Bermuda shorts.

We burst out laughing. Braided Beard Guy jumped up, took a bow, and pranced off through the seething mass of humanity on the boardwalk.

Junior passed Rasta the twenty dollar bill he had earned cleaning graffiti. “What should we do with it?”

“Go buy yourself dinner, maybe put a deposit on a battery for David’s van.” They bounded away like puppies.

“Speaking of dinner.” My stomach was gurgling in a loud, really unattractive way. John looked at me and smiled. He packed up his art and set out his crowns. Some surfers strolled by and admired his handiwork.

“How much, man?”

“Well, you know, I like to get my fifteen dollars.”

They shook their heads. The younger one pulled out a five dollar bill.

“I only got five.”

“Sold!”

They smiled, thrilled at their score. John pocketed the cash. I was flabbergasted. "Why did you sell it for five? How will you ever get off the street if you kept under pricing yourself?

"Fast nickel's better than a slow dime."

I slid into my marketing android mode, "If you want to get ahead, you've got to stick to your price!"

He turned slowly and looked at me. "Okay, Miss University degree, what could you do, right now, to make money for dinner?"

I shifted uncomfortably. I couldn't think of anything. I'd been in the same clothes for three days, no shower, no soap, scared to even guess what my hair looked like hidden under my hat. And I'm sure I had a really tantalizing fragrance going on under my armpits.

"Nothin."

"Hello."

As we packed up I gently touched his arm. "Sorry."

"Nothin to it," was his soft reply. The smile told me he wasn't mad. We headed out, Rasta John's collection of bags hanging off of him. Wherever he went, his entire home went, he was a human RV. We turned off the boardwalk onto Rose and headed inland to Main Street. On Main John turned north and pointed us toward Santa Monica.

"Where are we going?"

"A health food store that was one of my customers when I was growing wheat grass."

"You grew wheat grass?"

"After I heard Ann Wigmore give a lecture on how wheat grass healed her after doctors wrote her off, I set up a dome and grew flats of wheat grass. Brought them to the natural food stores every day. When my mom was dying of a brain tumor back on Long Island, I flew home with some seeds. Military doctors sent her home to die, all bald, three big ole holes drilled in her head. I grew a flat of wheat grass and juiced it for her in our old meat grinder. We'd drink wheat grass and crochet every day. It cured her. I came back to L.A. but my old man kept feeding her fat, meat, donuts; managed to kill her anyway. And now, I make money crocheting crowns for dreads. She's still with me."

We arrived at the health food store and walked into a garden paradise. The air was full of the scent of fresh fruits, vegetables, wooden crates, and hardwood floors. The old wooden building was like a warm hug. I just stood for a moment and let it wash away the street grime.

John motioned for me to follow him to the juice bar. For a dollar he bought us each an ounce of wheat grass juice. He handed me a lemon wedge to bite into to cut the grass taste.

The last few days with very little to eat gave me a real appreciation for something as pure as wheatgrass. The juice shot through my blood system like an espresso. I felt my sinuses open up, and all the pistons in my brain start firing.

John moved through the aisles, carefully picking out what dinner we could afford with the remaining four dollars. He purchased a container of alfalfa sprouts, a beautiful tomato, and a small jar of artichoke hearts. At the cashier, he picked up two plastic forks and some napkins. People working in the store nodded at the dread, recognizing him from years of collaboration; sadness in their eyes for his plight.

As we headed back up Main Street John paused in front of a giant mural gracing the side of a building. “That’s me.”

I stepped closer and sure enough, hidden behind the pay phone at the corner of the building, was his signature, John Warner Scott. I stepped back and admired the mural. How many other pieces of art had I admired without knowing that the talent behind it could be homeless?

“Why did they have to put that phone right there?” He touched his signature and shook his head. It was my first look at his portfolio, and I was impressed.

Back on the boardwalk, the air was crisp and fresh after the rain. Even the *eau de beach* had been washed away. We sat together at a picnic table and John prepared our meal. He opened the sprout container and tore off the lid, making two dinner plates. He carefully cut the tomato into pieces and put half on each bed of sprouts. The artichoke hearts followed, topped off with the marinade from the jar. He pushed one toward me.

“Give praise and thanks,” we chorused and dug in. It was the best tasting meal I could remember. A soft rain began to fall again and he talked without looking up from his dinner.

“You know, we could dig a wider trench and both sleep under my tarp tonight to stay dry.”

I could feel him holding his breath. I felt a warm rush of energy around me. The thought of sleeping with John in his nest of warm blankets under a rain proof covering was the equivalent of the Hilton compared to my one blanket in the soggy sand.

"That would be great!"

He smiled and nodded; too shy to look my way. We ate in silence as the last daylight slipped away and the street lights came on. I remembered how late it was the previous night before we were able to sneak out to the wall, and I wasn't looking forward to a soggy evening of the same. We threw away our dishes and waited. Suddenly the power went out, all the street lights went dark, and there wasn't a roller in sight.

"Let's do it!"

We took off across the sand. This time I was a little faster and managed to keep within spitting distance of him, but I was still breathless by the time we dropped behind the wall. As soon as we did, the street lights came back on. We looked at each other and grinned. The Cosmos was working with us.

We began digging our trench. Within minutes we had the trench dug, lined, and climbed in. John lay on his back, stiff as a board. I snuggled next to him, but he remained rigid.

"You okay?"

He shook head. "Growing up, my old man used to beat me if he saw me talking to a white girl. I feel like his hand's gonna come flying out of the sky and smack me."

Wasn't racism dead? After the sixties with all the hippies protesting, flower children, peace and love, I thought we were all one big happy family. This was the eighties for heaven's sake!

"Nothing's changed. America's still racist. I was an art student in Kansas City when the Kansas City riots broke out. Same thing's ready to happen here thirty years later."

How prophetic his words would become. Four years later the famous Rodney King beating by police was caught on video tape by an amateur videographer in Los Angeles. The black community rioted, and Los Angeles burned.

"It's a trip."

"What?"

"I'm only part black. I got Irish, and Blackfoot Indian in me. But this is America. You got one drop of black blood in you, you black."

"Like Bob Marley."

"Yeah, like Marley."

We lay like that for a long time, pondering a world where we couldn't be friends without people being angry at us. A cloud circled the full moon overhead, and for a moment I could have sworn it resembled the symbol of the Rastafarian lion.

The lion next to me threw down the gauntlet. "So, you want to see it all?"

I knew what he was talking about. He'd seen me writing everything down, talking to the homies, trying to understand this world where white people feared to tread. "Yes."

"Then I'm your ticket." He rolled over and fell asleep.

Lying in the sand that August night in 1988, Existence heard me. It knew I was ready to have the blinders torn off my eyes. I was ready to learn the truth about life. And it was going to give me one hell of a ride.

7

JOY

I slept so soundly, warm, dry, hidden in the Earth, that I was completely revived by dawn. It was a beautiful sunny day, clear blue sky, the ocean quietly rolling next to us like a giant generator powering the world. I couldn't remember being this excited about a new day in a long time.

What a change. I remembered lying in bed when I was married, realizing in a cold, detached kind of way that it might be a blessing not to wake up. I really didn't care if I died; life had become so devoid of meaning. Working to pay the bills, to work to pay the bills couldn't be our higher purpose. Maybe that's why so many people with money, but no purpose, become addicts: alcohol, drugs, sex, anything to fill the monotony of living. Now, here, lying in the sand, I was excited about life again.

We did our morning recon for rollers. Two cruisers had stopped on the empty boardwalk while the police had a leisurely chat. I was beginning to understand why John was so patient, he had no choice. There was nothing we could do but wait.

As Buddha said, "*Do you have the patience to do nothing?*"

The rollers finally slid off the boardwalk and we sprang out of the earth. Worldly possessions in hand we headed to the pagoda fondly referred to as Mount Sinai. The rest of the camp emerged ninja-like from unfathomable hiding places in the blink of an eye. When the cruisers reappeared a minute later, the boardwalk was magically full of homies.

I could see the confusion in the policemen's eyes thinking, "Where the hell do they come from?"

Happy arrived with a newspaper and we all shared it, commenting on the news of the day. There were indeed more rumors that Carlos, the assassin, was in Los Angeles, and the homie hot line was sure he was on the beach.

"How could that be? Wouldn't the police find him?"

The beach was crawling with police, you'd think finding one of the world's most dangerous men would be a priority.

"This is the perfect place to hide. They don't care who we are, just something to be controlled, not understood, or identified," responded Happy. "They would be shocked if they knew who was hiding on this beach."

A local couple strolled by, out for a coffee, when the man looked over and recognized Rasta John. "Whoa, dude! I thought you were dead! How are you?"

"Dealin' with it."

"But you don't even have any scars! Man, when that dog mauled you, I thought you were history!"

"Jah watches over me."

The man shook his head. They high-fived and the couple moved away, the man looking back at John every few feet.

"What was that all about?"

"Couple of weeks ago I was meditating on the beach at dawn. A guy was walking his Rottweiler without a leash. It got away from him and ran at me. I thought of running, but something in my head said sit. So I did. When the dog got next to me it jumped over me and kept running down the beach. But that guy saw the dog maul me."

"What do you mean he saw you get mauled?"

"That's what matched his reality. I believed I was safe, he didn't. We saw what we each expected to see; Einstein's theory of relativity."

How many fights had I had with my ex, each of us adamant our memory of an event was the right one? I remember screaming in frustration about something he had done, which he swore he hadn't. Were we all living in alternative universes? Each of us floating in a bubble of our own creation, slamming into other people's bubbles, then fighting about whose bubble was real?

I thought about our Schizophrenic youth, Rikki. Who was I to say my world was more real than his?

*****

The rhythm of the days on the beach were the gentlest I had ever experienced. The Daily Prophet's chalkboard at the Breakfast club was an endless stream of inspiration. This morning it was a message from Gandhi, "*The more one suffers, the more one helps. The purer the suffering, the greater is the gain.*"

A boardwalk resident with a ground level apartment made a habit of putting his television in the window, facing out, so the homies could keep abreast of important events in the world. Today, it was a presidential debate.

The crowd gathered and helped set up the TV. A piece of cardboard was taped to the sides with duct tape, shading it from the sun and offering a bit more clarity to the screen.

The theatre completed, the homie crowd settled in for the show, hooting and hollering, clapping for their favorite, booing at the opponent.

Mom arrived and handed back everyone's neatly folded laundry. Junior showed up, shirtless and barefoot, with Rikki in tow.

John looked at him in exasperation. "Where are your shoes?"

Junior looked down at his feet in surprise and shrugged. N.Y. approached wearing an expensive track suit, carrying a tray of coffees and handed one to each of us. He had spent a wild night at a house party and was telling us stories when we heard a bright, cheery "Good Morning!"

We looked around, but couldn't find the source of the voice. Then we heard rustling overhead and looked up into the slats of the roof above us. It was Cuba. He had dragged a large cardboard box up into the slatted roof of the pagoda and made himself a type of tree house.

He waited for an all clear, then dropped down onto the table. He had ditched the expensive suit and was wearing a T-shirt and sweats. "I love it here! I'm never leaving!"

"Nobody back home's gonna miss you?" asked John.

He looked around nervously. "I left a situation back there. I won't be going back for a long time." He saw the roller blade concession opening up. "Gotta go! Got a job at the rental shack." And he was gone.

"What do you think happened in Cuba?" I asked the group.

"I'm thinking mob," said N.Y.

"I bet he got a girl pregnant," Junior, knowingly. And another debate was launched.

I looked over at John. "How's your art coming?"

John pushed it toward me and everyone crowded around to look.

N.Y. looked at him with new respect. "Wow, you're really good!"

Angel sauntered over, ready to hit on the men for cash, but she couldn't get their attention away from the art on the table.

Junior nudged her. "Have you seen the art he's doing for the Jamaican?"

She peered over Junior's shoulder at it. She looked at John and saw him for the first time. "You really are quite a catch, aren't you?"

John sighed.

She seemed to drift to another time, when she valued people for who they were, then quickly snapped out of it. "Can you spot me a twenty?"

He shook his head.

"Well, I think I'll head up to the Santa Monica camp, see what kind of action's going on."

She yanked on her top to display more cleavage, hiked up her short shorts, and was gone.

"Quite a catch," I mimicked.

"Jesus could walk up to her and offer her paradise but she be so busy showing off those nasty pants and asking for twenty dollars, she'd miss him. I been on this beach for two years, and suddenly, cuz you're with me, I'm a catch. She ought a quit."

"Yeah, she's a trip," agreed Junior.

John whirled around to face him. "I bet you ain't made any money today."

Junior shrugged and pretended to be absorbed with a blister on his sunburned body.

"Why don't you grab your guitar and go play for the tourists?"

Junior shrugged again, grabbed his guitar from Happy's "library and overnight storage" and wandered over to the Sidewalk Café. We moved closer. Live music was the best entertainment available on the beach.

Junior tuned his guitar, then began strumming Leonard Cohen's *Bird on a Wire.* He played with all his heart, but nobody paid any attention. Men in suits at the outside café tables held their newspapers closer to their faces, brilliantly Botox'd women chatted over croissants, while Junior played on, third person invisible.

John shook his head. "He's gotta give them a hint."

He took off his crown, formed it into a neat bowl shape, and put it on the sidewalk in front of Junior. He took a quarter out of his pocket, held it high for all to see, and ceremoniously dropped it into the hat. Junior sang with renewed hope. We all watched expectantly; still no response from the suits.

A lonely old woman shuffled by in her worn pink floral house dress. She had fuzzy slippers on her feet and tensor bandages wrapped around her ankles. A torn slip peeked out below the dress. She had on a man's forest green cardigan sweater; the front pockets weighted down with treasures. Woolen mittens adorned her hands.

She stopped in front of Junior and jammed her mitts into the pockets of her house dress. She struggled to pull them back out, lifting her dress up high, showing off a dazzling slip of torn lace. She wrestled with the dress for a moment, and finally freed her hands. Her fists held all the contents of her pockets. She leaned over the crown on the ground and released two fistfuls of change and lint. All her worldly goods donated for a song. She shuffled away.

Junior's voice soared over the palm trees. "*I saw a beggar, leaning on his wooden crutch. He called out to me, don't ask for so much!*"

Finally, the businessmen at the café were humbled. As they left with their cappuccinos, no-foam lattes, and newspapers, they dropped their extra change into Junior's hat.

A war veteran rolled past Junior and stopped at our table to catch up on news. He was in a wheelchair with a tiny kitten sitting on his shoulder. His skin was tanned and cracked like old leather after years in the Vietnam jungle, followed by more years on the beach. His blond hair was long and straggly, as was his beard. He wore his combat shirt from Vietnam. Old jeans barely hid the atrophying legs inside.

"Hey," he greeted us softly.

"One love, Brother."

He and John each pulled out a cigarette stub and lit up, enjoying the camaraderie of a shared smoke.

"How's it hanging, man?" asked the G.I.

"Dealin' with it. Hey, you ever tried to push that thing?" John pointed at the wheelchair.

"Never thought of it."

"I heard that cocaine steals calcium out of your bones. I'd jump back off that stuff for a minute if I was you, might be slowing your healing."

The G.I. nodded thoughtfully.

"You still taking the bus to the V.A.?" asked John.

"All they do is issue me horse tranquilizers. I can't function on the street taking those."

He saw a tourist drop a pizza box in a nearby trash can and quickly wheeled over. Half a pizza was still inside. He pulled off a piece of salami and fed it to the kitten, then put the box on his lap and wheeled away.

"What's the V.A.?" I asked John.

"Veteran's Administration hospital. Their idea of rehab is tranquilizing us 'til we die. Only thing those pills are good for is selling them for cash so's we can buy something useful."

"Who buys them?"

"Rich kids like to get high on those tranquilizers. Ain't that a trip?"

"Hey look!" yelled Mom, "Viva Zapata is on with Marlon Brando!"

The presidential debate had ended on Beach TV, and a movie was playing.

I turned in time to hear Brando say, "*You know it's not nice to kill crazy people.*"

A roar of approval went up from the homie crowd.

*****

Late afternoon found us in the throws of a major "happening". A spontaneous drumming circle erupted around one of the benches along the boardwalk. Condo dwellers came out with their expensive, imported African drums, while the homies used plastic two gallon buckets turned upside down.

Historically drumming has always been used to help people get closer to their God; Africans, Indians, ancient Romans. This lazy afternoon in Venice, California, it helped all of us express unfettered joy. We attracted tourists, locals, the police, and a virtual potpourri of humanity.

That's when the Crazy Brit decided to make an appearance. I glanced up in time to see her making a beeline for us. She was charging down the boardwalk in full glory: shirt billowing behind her like a cape, tits swinging. Some of the older tourists quickly turned and left. The locals glared at her, but the drummers ignored her, concentrating on the beat.

"What the fuck are you staring at?" the She Devil bellowed.

The crowd became skittish, ready to evaporate. I realized something had to be done, in a language she could understand, probably by another tall, blond member of the Commonwealth: Moi.

I stomped over to her and hissed into her ear. "Listen to me you two bit whore. These men have done nothing to you. No one came here to listen to you. So shut up or fuck off."

She whirled around and we stared; sunburned eyeball to sunburned eyeball. She might have been me when she first arrived, and I think she knew it. Her mouth clanged shut. She grabbed a large tattooed man and dragged him away.

A smattering of applause followed me as I went back to sit with John who couldn't hide the smile spreading across his face. I had officially earned my spot with the camp.

The Poet leaned close. "I got no sympathy for that woman. She's evil. If you saw the Devil lying on the side of the road, bleeding from his eyes, ears, and nose, and you KNEW it was the Devil, would you stop and help him?

I shook my head "No".

"No! If I saw someone flip her a quarter, I'd race her for it."

The drumming intensified until it reached a dramatic climax. The crowd clapped and cheered, dropping donations into one of the buckets as they left.

John handed back his bucket, knuckle knocked with the other drummers, and came over to the Poet. "You seen David?"

"Heard he was doing Supremes over at Four Corners last night."

"I better go find him. He was supposed to use that money to fix his van. You ready?"

I nodded. We were finally heading into the belly of the Beast.

8

FOUR CORNERS

"Watch for my signal, if I do this with my hand, stay back. We're going where they'll kill you for being white, so don't be doing your ballsy mountain girl routine."

We headed to Four Corners, the largest drug trafficking area in Los Angeles. It was a war zone. The air was thick with tension. Shadows behind barred windows watched us pass by. There was an energy in the neighborhood I had felt once before: at the German concentration camp in Dachau. This was the energy of the Hood; Hell on Earth.

There was nothing green here; all the small bungalows had barred windows and doors. There was no architectural design to speak of, just grey boxes housing grey souls. It looked like the inside of a penitentiary. In sharp contrast scores of children were riding brightly colored bicycles towards us.

"Where do these kids come from?"

"Early warning system for the crack houses."

Several children circled us, then sped down the street.

"They're warning the crack heads that you're here."

"Why would kids help crack heads?"

"Crack houses filter money down to the neighborhood. Some of these kids be living in cars with their mommas. Only money they see is from drug dealers. Who do you think they're gonna be loyal to? A system that ignores them, or someone who kicks them down cash every day?"

We rounded a corner lined with chain link fence. Two pit bulls hit the fence next to my face, barking hysterically. I lurched and fell back into John, heart thudding in my sweaty chest. Stone stares from several men on the porch of the house followed me, Oozy machine guns lazily aimed in my direction. John approached the fence and held up his finger.

"One love, Brothers, one love."

The guns lowered. The men nodded and moved back into the shadows of the porch. The pit bulls followed us the length of the fence, frenetic at their inability to rip me into bite size pieces. My heart was pounding so hard I could hear it in my ears.

"You okay?"

I nodded dumbly and a strange squeak escaped my constricting windpipe.

"Millions of dollars in rock cocaine is sold here every night. Street kids make money selling Macadamia nuts to high rollers that come down from the hills. Fools can't tell a nut from a rock."

I looked up to where Beverly Hills and Hollywood Hills hovered in the smoggy sky. I had been at homes in those hills, and never thought twice about what was going on down here.

We came abreast of a small bungalow with a crowd of men out front. John dropped his hand, palm facing back toward me. I froze. The men stared at me, oozing hate. John approached them, talked quietly for a moment, then returned.

“They saw David last night, this way.” The sun was setting. John picked up the pace. “We gotta get you out of here before dark.” And as an afterthought, “I hope that child is still alive.”

We moved through the streets, impending doom followed. John moved close to the buildings like a ninja and we slowly approached the famous intersection known as “Four Corners”.

Ahead of us police cruisers and black, unmarked DEA vans blocked the road. People were running, shouting, screaming. Their voices bounced off the walls of the barren landscape, matching the staccato bursts of the gunfire coming from a window high up in the apartment building. Police crouched down behind their cruisers, weapons drawn. And there, in the middle of it all, sitting on a bench eating popcorn, was Mom, the laundry lady.

John slid onto the bench next to her. “Hey, Sugar, what you doin’ out here?”

I dropped down low behind the bench as a police cruiser sailed by us, siren wailing. An unmarked car followed and screeched to a halt a few feet away from us. Men jumped out, DEA emblazoned on the back of their wind breakers.

“This is better than *Miami Vice*!”

Mom laughed and stuffed another handful of popcorn into her mouth. Her bravery and ability to laugh at life reminded me of my grandmother. She had survived an attack by a stalker when she was a nursing student in 1907. He ripped her face to shreds with a scalpel, then shot her several times before he slit his neck and died at her feet. She had fled to the Yukon where everyone from the gold rush was scarred.

I was lucky enough to know her when I was young. She had endured so much, seen behind the façade of it all, that in her twilight years she found life to be pretty hilarious. We'd sit in her room watching professional wrestling and she'd laugh until she cried. This homeless laundry lady reminded me of that gentle soul.

"You seen David?"

She nodded, "I sat here watching out for him until the Poet came and took him."

John smiled at her affectionately and shook his head, "You be careful out here. These cats is crazy!"

They shared a laugh and we were on the move again. We exited the Hood and made our way to Pacific Avenue. Back on the boardwalk, I slumped onto a bench, the nervous energy that kept me running had left me and I was suddenly exhausted.

"Do you think David will ever fix his van and get out of here?"

"Don't know."

"Seems like an easy solution."

"When you grow up in an insane asylum, even the simple solutions become impossible."

9

A NEW REALITY

We woke early to the peaceful surge of the ocean. I was now a seasoned pro when it came to rising like Lazarus in the morning and getting out of harm's way before the tractor chugged onto the sand.

John and I walked along the ocean's edge, enjoying the peace before the circus began. Using his finger, he began drawing in the sand, a large, circular mandala. I had never seen one before and asked him what he was doing.

"It's a meditation mandala. The circle is symbolic of the universe. Carl Jung drew one every morning in his notebook. It helped him focus."

"What are you focusing on?"

"Getting paid by that knucklehead for my art."

"Should that be a problem?"

"He always finds reasons not to pay me. I've cleaned that pigsty of his for years, just so I could have somewhere to sleep in the rain. Makes it impossible to come up with first, last and a damage deposit, hear what I'm saying?"

John stared out at the ocean. "Lots of people like to keep homies curbed; it's cheap labor for them. They know we have no legal recourse if they don't pay. People in society talk about having hard times, having their back against the wall. Well, then, I must be inside the wall."

I had never heard it put quite that way. To be so deep in despair that you feel trapped inside a wall. Yet, they carried on, these modern nomads, these discards of society. They had no choice.

I admired the intricate mandala he had drawn, "It's beautiful."

"The Buddhist Monks in Tibet create mandalas using colored sand for their sacred ceremonies. When the ceremony is over, they destroy the art, symbolizing the impermanence of life."

"You know a lot about Buddhism."

"I was Buddhist for ten years before I became Rasta."

As we stood on the shoreline *Day-Glo* pink jet streams shot across the sky, announcing the coming Sun. John turned to face it and closed his eyes in reverence, "Bullion".

A huge wave rolled in and swept away the mandala. Impermanence.

*****

We began our slow stroll to the Breakfast Club. A huge ball of seaweed washed up on the beach in front of us. It looked like a dead seal was wrapped up in it until I saw the ankle bracelet. Nausea surged in my throat. We stepped closer. John gently moved some seaweed to the side with his foot. The unmistakable zigzag scar on her face was gray beneath the tangle of blond hair. It was Angel. John grabbed my arm and steered me away as fast as he could without breaking into a jog.

"Wait, she might be alive," I sobbed.

He shot me a look that said I had rocks in my head. "American law says first black man on the scene is guilty."

"But I'll tell them you were with me!"

The reality of what I had just seen was making my world spin in a queasy "I've gotta sit down fast" way. We hurried to Mount Sinai where the camp was beginning to assemble. I sat on a bench with my back to the group and put my head between my knees. I didn't know whether to puke or pass out.

John motioned the camp to move in close and filled them in, "Angel just washed up on the beach."

He gestured to the spot and everyone looked. I looked too and was relieved to see a jogger guiding some policemen over to the pile of seaweed. They were questioning him intently, and I realized it probably was better that someone who wasn't a homie reported it.

The camp immediately started analyzing this new development with Angel.

"Well, you know who did it, don't you?" hissed the Poet. "She was up at the Santa Monica camp last night, stealing two and three dollas from men who only gots two or three dollas."

The camp nodded in agreement. Karma had hit. Apparently she would party with the ex-cons until they fell asleep and then go through their pockets. She did it one too many times and they snapped. The homie telegraph would know the culprit by the evening.

Silent signals were exchanged, apparently communicating my fragile state. Poet pulled out his radio cassette player. He turned it on, nothing happened.

Everyone rummaged through their bags until four AA batteries were found. The old batteries were replaced and he turned it on again. The morning traffic report filled the air.

"A car has driven off the freeway into the bushes. Southbound San Diego at Century is backed up to the Marina. There is a doghouse in the middle of Santa Monica Westbound," droned the announcer.

Everyone grinned and leaned in close; the World Series of rush hours.

"The Golden State is backed up from Glendale through Burbank. There's a rubbish fire at Ontario. A two car collision is blocking the Hollywood Freeway. The drivers are out of their cars engaged in fisticuffs."

"They ought a quit." John shook his head. The Poet giggled with glee and turned up the volume.

"There's something blocking 91. They're trying to get it off the road, it's a cow."

Wild cheering erupted from the camp.

*****

Another blissful day of art, conversation, and laughter slid by. A neighbor let us have a shower, and suddenly, I didn't feel quite so 'homeless'. As dusk started to settle onto the boardwalk and the tourists made their way back to the safety of their hotels, I prepared for another long wait to go to bed. Instead, a celebration began materializing.

Without a word, people congregated on the sand and built a bonfire. Word spread down the beach and in no time people arrived with guitars, drums, shakers, and beer. We threw everything that wasn't nailed down onto the fire.

An older dread with grey hair and wise eyes arrived with two younger dreads carrying the largest drum I had ever seen. It was a bass drum, handmade, about four feet across covered in goat skin. They set it on its side. The elder dread sat in front of it. He produced a huge mallet and started a slow, strong beat resembling a heartbeat. It was the beginning of a sacred drum session known as *Nyambingi* drumming.

Slowly, the other drummers joined in until the entire beach was pounding out a massive heartbeat of rhythm. Dancers got up and slowly moved around the fire, swaying in time to the drumming and the ocean. Black, white, yellow, mocha; every skin tone participated in this sacred fire ceremony.

I put my hand to my chest and felt my pulse beating to the rhythm. I looked over at John. His hands caressed a beautiful Djembe drum, he swayed to the beat, eyes closed, and slid into an ecstatic trance. It was the happiest I had seen him.

Spiritual texts talk about Maya, the delusion that we are all separate, that we stumble through life as islands, afraid, uncertain, alone. They talk about rising above Maya to realize we are one big spider web of humanity. A vibration in one part of the web creates ripples through the entire web. That night, I finally escaped the delusion of Maya, and experienced union. All our hearts were beating as one. I never wanted that night to end.

We played the sun down into the ocean. We played the stars up into the sky. And I swear to God Existence winked at me.

10

THE ARTIST'S WAY

"I want to take you somewhere special today." John's whole body language had changed. He seemed more relaxed, more sure of himself. I liked it.

"Like a date?"

He grinned shyly and nodded. "We deserve a treat, and I got to get out of the mix for awhile."

Sales of his crowns had gone well, and he wanted to spend the money on us. I was touched. Without telling me our destination, he led me away from the beach.

We walked North on Ocean Avenue to Wilshire and turned inland. Wilshire is one of those majestic streets that takes you through the heart of the metropolis. It connects five of the major business districts with each other. The arrogant high rises we passed were testament to that. As the sun lazily made its way higher in the sky, I felt like a kid on a family road trip. "Are we there yet? I'm tired. I have to pee."

Finally we stopped in front of the biggest mud puddle I had ever seen. "This is it? This is what you dragged me across town to see?"

He laughed and shook his head. He pointed to a nearby building: The Los Angeles County Museum of Art. Ah, now that made sense. But I had to take one more look at the puddle. We were facing the famous paleontology site known as the La Brea Tar Pits, where prehistoric animals had become trapped in tar (*La Brea* in Spanish) millions of years ago.

This was just so "Hollywood". I could see the city planners huddled around a boardroom table, "Okay, what are we missing? Oh, I know, fossilized remains of Mastodons in the middle of the financial district. Brilliant!"

We walked over to the Art Museum and John nonchalantly headed up the front steps. I couldn't follow him. I was suddenly self conscious of the "homie" ensemble I was wearing. Sure, I was cleaner since yesterday's shower, but I was still in beach wear, not appropriate for viewing millions of dollars worth of art. Well dressed men and women were walking into the building, and I was standing there like a vagabond. I told John I didn't think I could do it.

"Don't be trippin'. They'll think you're an artist."

I took a deep breath and we walked up the steps and into the foyer. John paid for two admissions, winked at me, and we entered. Immediately we were confronted by a massive abstract by Jackson Pollack and my art history lesson began. I stared at what looked like someone vomiting rainbows.

"Alcoholic," muttered John. "Luckily he found a good woman to keep him on track."

We moved through majestic rooms with high ceilings and the most amazing art collections I had ever seen. We passed a painting called *The Cotton Pickers* by Winslow Homer depicting Southern Blacks.

John held up his index finger and offered a silent "One Love".

We moved on past a George Wesley Bellows painting of the homeless and John spoke so softly I could barely hear him, "My man."

Next was a room of landscapes. John moved over to a modest size painting depicting a cottage in the country. "What do you think?"

"It's alright," I shrugged.

"Well, homeboy spent a couple of years on that 'alright painting'. It's made of tiny tiles."

I looked closer and sure enough, it wasn't a painting it was a mosaic of tiles barely bigger than grains of sand. "Why would someone do that?"

"You KNOW they took him away in a straight jacket."

We moved from room to room to room, and the commentary became more and more depressing.

"Went insane, died a pauper, cut off his ear..."

John's years at the Art College in Kansas City had taught him the sad truth. Art investors would make the money, while most artists would probably live as paupers and die unknown.

We arrived back at the Jackson Pollack painting at the front entrance. John stood staring at it a long time.

"I met his wife, Lee Krasner. She said I had the gift. I was working at a gallery in New York as a framer. She came into the back to thank me and saw some of my work."

"Did she offer to help you sell it?"

"No time. She was a great artist herself. Busy managing Pollack's estate. Let's eat."

We bought some sandwiches and drinks in the cafeteria, and went outside to the patio. I felt worlds away from the beach, and from my life before the beach. We were in an alternate dimension; a painting of our own creation. I asked him what inspired his art.

He spoke quietly, always aware that he was on display. People were watching him, judging every move he made. The lone black man in a very white world.

"I was born blind. My mom prayed over me until I could see. They say that's the sign of a seer. I don't know about that, but all my art comes to me in dreams. Sometimes I don't even sign my paintings, They aren't mine, I'm just the messenger."

We ate in silence for a while, then he spoke so softly I could barely hear him.

"I had a vision that a woman from another country was coming to take me off the beach."

I held my breath.

"I been asking around, and I know a roller blader got a place up in Topanga Canyon he never uses, said I could rent it from him for $200, same as what the Jamaican said he'd pay for the cover art. We could go stay there."

That voice in my head told me this was the one I'd been searching for the minute we met on the beach. The feeling had been growing every minute I was with him. I was blown away by his kindness, his integrity, his ability to bring joy to impossible situations.

The people on the beach depended on him, and he was asking me to trust him.

I believe in reincarnation, and I had the strongest feeling that we had been together before, that we had meant a lot to each other in another lifetime. There was no other explanation for the immense sense of belonging that I had with him.

I had to make a decision. There's no way to date a homie, no way to call him up, leave a message, meet for a casual coffee. I knew that once I left the beach, I would never see him again. I wasn't ready to let that happen.

"Let's do it," I said.

He broke into a massive smile. We toasted with our juice boxes. The next thought that sprang into my head was, "*All hell is going to break loose*!"

I had no idea how right I would be.

*****

We now walked in unison, a result of miles and miles covered together. I wondered if our hearts were beating in time like the Nyambingi heartbeat. *Miles to go before I sleep* flitted through my mind. I wondered if the person who wrote that had been homeless.

When we arrived at the beach we didn't have to do the usual wait to run for the wall. The Crazy Brit was screaming obscenities, and keeping both police cruisers busy. We took advantage of the distraction and ran for it. As we were about to crawl into our trench a skinny, young white man hurried over to John.

"Hey, you got a joint?" His eyes glowed white in the moonlight while his body nervously fidgeted and jerked.

"Man, I ain't got nothin' for you."

"Aw, come on man, I haven't slept in days!"

He was almost hysterical, and I could smell him from several feet away. John dragged him down behind the wall, out of view of rollers.

"Look at you, all wide eyed, hip hoppin' around, and sweatin' like a pig. If you ain't a trip!"

"I just need a joint so I can sleep."

John looked around, then pulled a joint out of his Keds sneaker. "You need to back off that crack. A body can't stay up for days. I'll give you a hit, but don't say nothin' to me, you hear?"

The kid nodded, eagerly eyeing the joint. John lit it and passed it to him. The kid took two deep inhales, his eyes rolled up in his head, and he dropped to the sand with a whoof.

John shook his head, and gently pulled the joint out of the youth's immobile hand. He wet two fingers, snubbed it out, and carefully replaced it in his sneaker.

"Who knows, maybe a good night's sleep, he'll kick it. I don't like to see anyone that far out there." He crawled under the blankets. I was asleep before John pulled the blankets over our heads and covered us with sand.

11

PAY DAY

I woke up and watched the stars slowly melt into the morning Indigo sky. It's hard to describe how I felt - excited, scared, panicked, all at the same time. This was an even bigger leap of faith than I had planned when I arrived on the beach.

I had called a friend who lived near the beach and arranged for a ride the next morning. Today John had to get paid for his art, pay rent to the Roller Blader and get the key to the room in Topanga Canyon. Then there was the issue of having to say good bye to his camp. Seemed like an easy "To Do" list, but it was a virtual *Rubik's Cube* when you're homeless.

We sprouted from the sand like daisies and buried the blankets. The police had dragged away the young man during the night.

Only one more sleep to go. John went to the water's edge and drew his morning mandala.

"Forget that!" I drew a giant check in the sand for a million dollars. "We need to send a peace offering to the prosperity gods."

We said a prayer. A wave came in and wiped the slate clean. There was no Breakfast Club on the weekend, so we waited for the camp at Mount Sinai. Cuba dropped down out of the pagoda roof and joined us. His transformation was complete; he was now a full blown beach bum. His surfer shorts clashed loudly with a *Day-Glo* tank top, and flip flops.

"Where's all your luggage and expensive clothes?"

"Gave it all away to homies!"

We laughed at the vision of homeless men wearing thousand dollar designer suits.

"I've never felt this free, this happy!"

I knew what he meant; being around people who had no preconceived notions of who you were, or who you were supposed to be, was freeing. I realized I was being given an opportunity to reinvent myself away from the analytical stares of family, old friends, bosses. It was like being a kid again.

"Maybe we should start selling tickets", joked John. "Be a homie for twenty-four hours, guaranteed to cure all ills!"

Bit by bit the camp assembled; each wayward soul manifesting from the ethers. N.Y. strolled over with coffees. Happy arrived with the newspaper.

When everyone was present, John made the announcement, "We got a place in Topanga. We're leaving tomorrow."

The camp looked at us in wonder.

Junior's voice caught in his throat, "You're leaving?"

Junior and David were visibly shaken. John had been their surrogate father for a long time.

"Don't worry, I'll come down during the day to sell my crowns."

"You've changed the whole vibration on this beach," said Happy. "You've given people hope."

N.Y. stared at us and shook his head, "You two are really going to give it a shot? That's great!" He hugged us both. "I got to re-evaluate the way I date."

I laughed, but John was tense. "First, I got to get my money from the Jamaican."

The camp's enthusiasm hiccupped. John had been trying to get off the street for two years. He had produced concert posters, T-shirts, and album cover art for the Jamaican, and still the carrot dangled in front of his nose, just out of reach. The Jamaican had found the perfect balance with John, just how much praise, sprinkled with the right amount of abuse, to keep the artist's low self-esteem in check. The camp realized that our dream of leaving could evaporate like the morning mist.

John turned to David and Junior, "Watch my stuff."

The camp spread out the batik cloth and relaxed under the palm trees while John and I headed out.

Butterflies crashed around angrily in my stomach. I tried to put on a brave front, but the air was thick with foreboding. John needed to instigate his own escape from the street. Simply leaving with me, being indebted to me was a bad way to start any relationship and we both sensed it. We hurried down the alleys and through the streets, to grandma's house we went. Would the Big Bad Wolf be waiting there for us?

John knocked on the no frills door. "Hey, Man, open up, I got your art."

The Jamaican peered at us through the bars on the bedroom window. He and Indigo were still in bed.

“Wha?” mumbled the Jamaican.

John went to the window and leaned close, “I got your art.”

“Oh, yeah. Hey, you seen my parrot? Someone jus’ reach in de window and snatch de bird away. We heard his voice getting’ further an further away, like he was runnin’ down the alley.”

“No, man, I ain’t seen your bird.”

John rolled his eyes at me and went back to the door. The Jamaican pushed it open and stood there naked and arrogant, daring me to deny he was God’s gift to women. John handed over the art. The Jamaican flipped through the pages.

“Is beautiful, Mon. Hey Indigo, come look at dis.”

Indigo slid into view with a ratty bedspread wrapped around her like a cloak. She looked at the art, then at John. “Hey! You’re really good!”

“Been at it my whole life.”

“Could you, I mean, would you teach me? I can’t afford art school.” Indigo was once more the shy child she really was. She looked at John with new respect.

“Sure, Sweetie.”

My heart went out to her. Who knew what her home life had been like to make her run away so young; never graduate, never go to a prom, never see art college, and become the sex toy of this pervert. Here was a shot at a dream.

The Jamaican nodded and started to close the door. John knew the routine and got his foot in, blocking it.

"Hey, Man, we had a deal, two hundred dollars. You know that ain't much for full color seps like you got there. I got a chance at a room, hear what I'm saying?"

The Jamaican sized us both up and smirked. No one was getting off the street on his watch, especially none of HIS homies. Without slave labor, his empire would collapse, and he knew it.

"I'm broke. What you want me to do?" His look was cunning, the wolf peeking out from under grandma's bonnet.

"C'mon, Man. Don't do me like this. You always have that much cash lying around." John was trying not to crack under the strain of this bizarre negotiation.

I could feel my pulse pounding, at a loss for how to make this situation right. The Jamaican glared at John and kicked his foot out of the doorway, slamming the door shut. We stood in stunned disbelief.

"They ain't never gonna let me get off of this beach." John stood staring at the steel door.

I could feel his heart breaking. In the distance sirens wailed.

He knocked softly on the door again. "Hey Man, open up."

No response.

"I want my artwork back."

From inside we heard a muffled, "What?"

"I said gimme back my art!"

The Jamaican appeared at the bedroom window. "Who else you gonna sell it to? It's got my name on it."

"We'll burn it tonight to keep warm," growled John.

Both the Jamaican and I saw the lion emerge. Gone was the humble, mild mannered artist. In his place stood a Rastafarian Lion.

"I need it for my meeting tomorrow," whined the Jamaican.

"Then pay me!" John glared at the con man.

Finally the Jamaican disappeared from the window and rummaged around his bedroom. He reappeared at the front door and passed out a check. John took it. The door slammed shut. We both peered at the check. It was made out to John Scott, a man whose only I.D. was as a U.S. Army projectionist and no bank account.

Three, two, one...lift off. I lost my sunburned, righteous Canadian mind. I kicked and banged at the door, screaming at the top of my lungs. I wasn't a homie anymore, and I was damned if I was going to stay quiet.

"You know he can't cash a check like this you asshole!"

The commotion got the door open in record time. The Jamaican had only ever heard a handful of words from me, and the performance had the effect I was hoping for.

I shoved the check back at him. "No bank will let him cash this and you know it!"

The Jamaican took the check back and quickly produced a new one. "Make it out to whoever you want!"

He slammed the door. We were left holding a blank check for two hundred dollars. The Jamaican had finally paid, but it was too late to stop his downward spiral. His karma would catch up to him and within the year he would become one of the homeless on Venice Beach.

John looked at me in amazement, then back at the check. Tears filled his eyes. "No one ever stood with me before."

"I'm a regular rabbit's foot."

"I'm scared a you."

We moved away from the door and onto the street. The address for the bank was only a block away and we practically jogged there. John made the check out to "Cash" and emerged from the bank with two hundred dollars in his hands.

"This is it, isn't it? We're really leaving."

He looked at me with the eyes of a child who thinks Christmas may not be for real; may only be for kids in fancy neighborhoods with two sane parents and a pet pig.

"We're going to Topanga Canyon!" I hugged him. For the first time, we held hands and walked down the street.

"What the hell's she doing with you!?" screamed an angry looking white man. He was making a beeline across Main from the other side of the street, intent on getting in John's face.

"I said," he was now nose to nose with John, "what the hell's she doing with you?"

"I don't know," replied John, a look of wonder on his face.

The steam rushed out of the angry man's engine, confusion on his face. It wasn't the response he was hoping for. He wanted a fight. He wasn't prepared for this passive response. Gandhi would have been proud. The man slunk down the street.

I turned on John. "What do you mean you don't know why I'm with you? I love you! I wouldn't be doing all this if I didn't."

"I don't know why you're with me. Look at us. It makes no sense." We burst out laughing. We laughed all the way to the beach. Word spread like wildfire that the Jamaican had paid. We celebrated with an unheard of second cup of coffee. At the infamous take out window where Angry Man stood guard, he actually smiled. We ordered two coffees, and this time they came with creams, sugars, and more smiles. When John tried to pay him he waved it away.

"Good luck, you two." His voice caught in his throat. Was that a tear I saw glistening in his eye?

"These are the days of miracles and wonder," sang Paul Simon in my head.

We rejoined the group at the Sandominium and John was asked to recount over, and over, and over again exactly how he managed to get money out of the Jamaican. All kids have their favorite story. The story they never tire of because it makes them feel safe. For Junior, David, Happy, The Poet, Cuba, N.Y. and even Rikki, this was the story. It made them believe magical things could happen for them too.

I sat on the batik and watched them, my new family. In only a few days I had enveloped them the way I would a lover. My heart broke for them with each disappointment, each promise broken, every fraud reveled.

Finally, John got up. “Wait here, I’ll get our key.”

He gave me a kiss and the camp practically swooned. John waved and walked away. I blissfully sat on the knoll and watched the world make its lazy turn. Now that the work and struggle was done, my mind was a blank. I felt washed clean.

Everyone wandered off, looking for work, and I was left in the shade with Rikki and Happy. I got out my writing tools and made notes. Happy watched me from his chaise lounge. “Was it everything you thought it would be?”

“More.” I wrote for a bit, then put my pen down. “Happy, why are you here? You seem more like a professor on sabbatical than a homie.”

“I like to read,” was all he would reveal, smile crinkles winking at me.

“Why do you think Rikki is here?” We looked at the gentle soul playing with his imaginary friends.

“I’ve always been fascinated by the inner world of Schizophrenics, but Rikki is the first one I’ve been able to observe in the wild. Usually they’re so overmedicated you can’t see the personality hidden beneath. But Rikki is all…”

“Rikki,” we said in unison.

We watched him sitting on the batik, smiling at the waves, living in an existential world many dimensions away from us. I had a thought.

"You know, his world could be the real one, ours could be the delusion."

"Well, then, his world is as cruel as ours," said Happy. We both looked at Rikki's missing fingers.

"Happy, you said Laing believed that madness was a result of individuals being put in impossible situations with conflicting expectations, leading to a lose-lose situation. According to the Hindus we are in an Earth cycle right now called the "Kali Yuga", age of hypocrisy. If that's true, we'll probably be seeing more and more 'Rikkis' on the street."

"I daresay, we may."

Years later I became friends with two different women who were Schizophrenic. Both had parents who claimed they don't know why their daughters turned out this way, but it was obvious to anyone who heard their stories that the child was in an impossible situation.

One young woman was told everything was fine at home when she was young. She would come home from school and sit on a hill outside her house listening to her father beat her mother. One day, when she was finally old enough and big enough, she threw her father out. She had to protect the parent, her mother, who should have been protecting her. She had her first Schizophrenic episode shortly after.

The other patient was constantly being sexually harassed by her father's friends. He didn't believe her. She felt betrayed. She 'checked out' shortly after.

What had Rikki endured that drove him to the beach? "What will happen to him?" I couldn't bear the thought of Rikki jumping off a building without John there to stop him.

"I don't know. I don't know where his parents are. And if he was in a treatment facility, they would simply medicate him until he dies. There is no money in finding a cure; the money is in the treatment." Happy didn't look so happy anymore.

"I've heard of people who heal Schizophrenics in India. They can see that the physical and astral bodies of the person are out of alignment. They whack them at the top of the spine with a stick and cure them." I looked at Rikki, wondering if that would work.

"Sort of like Carlos Castaneda's shaman. He whacked him with a stick to fix aberrant behavior," he laughed.

Years later in Calgary I learned of a man who realized some people diagnosed as Schizophrenic were actually suffering from possession by a disembodied spirit. These spirits were most frequently hanging around hospitals, where their bodies had died, and they would prey on patients in weakened states. I met a woman who had become 'schizophrenic' after a hospital stay and after years of being medicated, was given an exorcism by this therapist and she was cured. She is now a health professional herself. Reality sure is a strange creature.

We sat with Rikki under the palm trees. From time to time he would get the giggles, giving Happy and me the giggles. It was one of those rarified moments in time when all feels right with the Cosmos. I felt God laughing with us.

As the sun started to go down, it was time for homies to change gear. Happy packed up his books and took them to the bike rental place to be locked up for the night. He took Rikki by the arm and they wandered off for dinner. I looked around the beach.

The tourists had left. My camp was off having adventures, and John was nowhere in sight.

12

LOST

Mom swung by to say good night, heading for her back porch. I asked her if she'd seen John, but she hadn't. I was worried. I couldn't go look for him or we could be running around, just missing each other, all night. One of us had to stay put, stay "home". I guess it was me.

She saw the look of panic on my face and sat down. "I guess I don't have to leave quite yet."

I smiled appreciatively. Here was my chance to hear her story.

"Do they call you Mom because you do their laundry, or because you have kids?"

"I do laundry in exchange for protection. It beats having to act crazy." She saw the blank look on my face and continued. "A woman on the street's gonna be raped sooner or later unless she's got a gimmick."

She jumped up, grabbed her crotch, and bounced around the sidewalk screaming. "Crabs! AHHH, Crabs!"

She stopped as fast as she'd started; a sheepish grin on her face. We both laughed. "If Rasta doesn't come back, you'll have to come up with something pretty quick."

"Like the Crazy Brit?"

She shrugged. We sat in silence until I couldn't take it anymore, my curiosity was killing me.

"How did you wind up here?"

She smiled a shy smile and shrugged. "It's not an extraordinary story. I lived in a house just a few blocks from here. I loved that place, worked hard to keep it nice, keep it a home. Then that lazy ass husband of mine took off, leaving me to raise four boys alone. Then the boys turned out to be as lazy as their father, lying sprawled on the sofas all day while I worked three jobs. I couldn't get them to help out. It was such a relief when they started moving out. I can still remember my last day in the house. My youngest son had finally moved out. I was done. I locked the door, cracked open a beer and put my feet up. Then I heard a loud banging on the door."

"It was my oldest. His girlfriend had thrown him out for being a lazy, no good, S.O.B. So he came back. Back to my front door, ready to become my burden again. I put down the beer, left the keys on the table, and jumped out the window. I've been living under my old back porch ever since."

"You live under your old home?"

She nodded, grabbed her bags, and headed out. "See you around, Canada."

She moved on, pushing her shopping cart. As the sound of the squeaking wheels faded I realized it was the first time I had felt completely alone on this beach; no camp to keep me company, no homies to tell me stories, just me.

I watched the dying colors of the day light the sky and reflected on what had been a perfect day. John had been paid, we had a place to move, both our lives were leaving their orbits and spinning off to circle a new Sun.

Now, all I could do was wait. But what if he didn't come back? What if he just took the money and left without me? My mind began to run amuck, and as always, I was hungry. If John was with me I knew what he'd say, "You're trippin". And I was.

The sky grew dark, and with it came the night creatures. This is where filmmakers get their inspiration for zombies, from watching crack addicts on Venice Beach. These were the walking dead. Bodies that hadn't slept for days were being driven around by demonic souls. I'd heard people talk about how crack was the "Jekyll and Hyde" drug. Normal people became demonic monsters when they've been using it for too long.

One theory is that the soul needs to get out of the body regularly, which is why we sleep. If you don't sleep for days, the soul leaves anyway, refusing to work overtime, and a "walk in" occurs. This is known in the metaphysical world as a soul that refuses to acknowledge it has died, and prowls around looking for a soul in a weakened state.

Now here I was, utterly alone, watching the undead prowl the boardwalk. A screaming, bloated woman came abreast of me. I quietly sunk back into the shadows. Her eyes were bloodshot, the few teeth in her head were yellow, and her belly was horribly distended. She clawed at her rotting arms. The voice coming out of her was deep, guttural, male. She spun around like a top, not knowing where to go, then collapsed onto a nearby bench.

This was why the Santa Monica camp of ex-cons was afraid to come down here. I had been blissfully unaware of it wrapped up in John's protective bubble. This was the malevolent side of Venice. I was looking around for a way to escape when a pack of fellow "zombies" appeared and dragged her away.

As they disappeared into the darkness, I noticed the television facing the boardwalk was still on. Just like a kid missing a parent, I plopped down in front of the set to drown out my loneliness. An interview with Mother Theresa was on, and she was looking straight at me.

"And if God puts you on the street, to accept being on the street. To accept whatever he gives you with a big smile. Surrender, then you are free."

I couldn't stop the tears from falling. I had asked for this, God had given it to me, and I was scared to death. A howling noise was coming out of a nearby alley so I grabbed our bags and walked out to the Wall. I sat with my back against it, unwilling to bury myself in the sand alone. I stared out at the waves, moonlight shining off them like jewels.

I had been sitting there for several freaked out hours when the commotion started. Hollering and shouting was bouncing off the deserted buildings along Ocean Front Walk. I peeked over the Wall. A crowd was approaching, and in the middle of it was John, handcuffed, flanked by two policemen.

Mom ran along beside them. "You've got the wrong man! John wouldn't hurt anybody!"

The large "Burley Cop" spun on her, "Back off, lady."

More homies yelled insults. The "Younger Cop" seemed uncomfortable with his role, but the Burley Cop kept pushing John along. John motioned toward the sand and they moved onto the beach, toward me. I stayed hidden in the shadows as the parade approached.

"What did he do?" yelled a homie.

"They think he's Enriquez," Mom answered.

When they got closer I could hear the conversation going on. The cops were breathing heavily, reminding me of my first hike onto the beach.

"Where did you say it was?" wheezed the Young Cop.

"I keep my I.D. buried out here in a bag." He was gliding across the sand as the policeman kept sinking with each step. Their breathing was labored as John came to a halt at the Wall. He saw me and nodded discreetly, then led the police away from me so I could get on the other side, out of view.

"I think it's over here, but I can't dig with these on."

They unlocked the handcuffs.

He dropped to the sand and dug. "Nope, maybe over here."

He crawled to another spot and dug. The police were bent over, hands on their knees, gasping for air while John went through his little treasure hunt. "Here it is!"

He had discreetly removed the wallet from its hiding place in his clothes and dropped it on the sand. I realized he wanted to get back to me any way he could, and showing his ID back in the hood might have prevented that. He straightened up and started the slow laborious process of sorting through the papers in his wallet while one the Young Cop shone his flashlight on it. Finally, John handed over his projectionist license from the U.S. Army. They looked at it then shone flashlights in his face.

"See?" he announced innocently, "Not Enriquez!"

"Spread 'em." The Burley Cop started patting him down.

The Younger Cop grew more uncomfortable. "He's not Enriquez, just leave him."

"Oh, he's guilty of something." He was itching for a cavity search. He made John take off his worn Keds. The stub of a joint fell out.

"Aha!!" Burley Cop triumphantly held the stub aloft for all to see.

"I must be Public Enemy Number One," said John.

"Shut up!" The cop kept searching. He pulled a small zip lock baggie out of one of John's pockets. "What do we have here? Cocaine?"

"Look at it, it's a jeweler's bag," sighed John.

They shone their flashlights on it, something delicate and silver glittered in the light. They shoved the bag back at him.

"We're watching you." Burley Cop did a lame commando move pointing his two fingers at his eyes, then at John's eyes. They stumbled away. Several homies came over and patted John on the back, congratulating him on a great performance. The entertainment value of this one would keep them laughing for weeks. As they melted into the dark I went over to him.

"You okay?"

He shook his head and we sat down, leaning against the wall. "I can't hang with this anymore."

"I thought you weren't coming back," I tried to be calm, but a sob escaped anyway.

He leaned over and kissed me. "I'm sorry, I wanted to surprise you."

"Well, ya did."

"My friend knows a jeweler in Mexico. He brings stuff across the border to sell. I was picking out a bracelet for you, when those two showed up." He opened the baggie and presented me with a delicate filigree silver bracelet.

I held it up in the moonlight. "It's beautiful!"

He helped me put it on. "I can't be calling you my girl without giving you something!"

It was such an old fashioned sentiment, and it touched me. My first husband hadn't even bothered with an engagement ring when we got married; said I could wear the washer and dryer on my ring finger.

We were both drained emotionally, and for the last time dug a trench and crawled into the earth. I stared at the stars in the sky and heard John, spooned up behind me, whisper in my ear, "Give praise and thanks".

13

LEAVING VENICE

The next morning slid onto the beach like a wave of hope. It was a still, peaceful day. The universe was holding its breath. And so was I. I'm sure my pounding heart was making the Earth spin a little quicker.

We gathered all our belongings, in John's case, all his earthly possessions, and walked to Mount Sinai to say goodbye to the camp. Everyone was in a melancholy mood; happy that we had found a home, sad that Rasta John wouldn't be traveling with them anymore.

N.Y. delivered our ceremonial tray of coffees in a business suit. After much whistling and lewd comments from the gang, he explained. "I'm heading back to New York."

"You can't leave now!" This from Cuba, "The party's just getting started."

"I've got a job back there. They'll never believe this!" N.Y. shook his head and laughed at our little troop.

The Poet came bounding up. "Did you hear? They caught Enriquez. He's Puerto Rican!"

Every black dread on the beach had been interrogated for something an olive skinned, blond dread had done. We sat discussing all of this beach news as Mom approached. But she wasn't Mom anymore. Gone were the beach clothes and shopping cart. She was in a dress and walking with an older woman.

“Hey, I’d like you to meet my Mom. She’s come to take me home.”

We were speechless. One by one the camp hugged the gentle woman who had “mothered” this group of men for so many years.

“It’s about time, Sweetie,” John whispered in her ear.

“How did this happen?” I asked.

“I finally called her.”

“All this time she didn’t know you were homeless?”

“I was too embarrassed to tell her.”

Her Mom came over and put her arm around her. “Thank you for taking care of my daughter.”

“Who’s gonna do our laundry?” whined Junior.

The Poet smacked him upside the head.

We waved at them as they left the boardwalk for good.

The Poet gave John an emotional hug. Who knows what they had been through together, but they had survived two years on the street and were ready to re-enter society.

He looked over at me, “You take care of my homeboy. He’s been waiting a long time for you.”

PART TWO:

A NEW LIFE

14

TOPANGA CANYON

Home became a tiny room above the Health Food store at the corner of Topanga Canyon and Fernwood Boulevards. It was a rustic old building that backed onto a steep hill. The Health Food store was run by a wonderful Asian man who let John help out at the store in exchange for groceries. John was in bartering heaven.

Topanga Canyon is located in the Santa Monica Mountains. Malibu sits at the Pacific Coast side of the Boulevard, and Ventura Highway joins the Valley side. We soon found it was just as rebellious as Venice Beach. It had a long list of famous musicians and artists living there, including Neil Young. Driving into the canyon we left the world of sidewalks, street lights, anything resembling Los Angeles, and entered a small town that could have been located in the Ozarks. Cabins perched on canyon walls glared down at us, daring us to stop.

Dozens of illegal grow ops were scattered up in the hills. John and I quickly learned that going for a walk in the neighborhood wasn't that different from the Hood, except instead of Crips wearing clan colors pointing Oozies at us; we had hippies in tie-dyed T-shirts with shot guns.

We didn't leave Venice Beach completely. Every day we drove down to the beach and John would sell his crowns and keep up his contacts for art jobs. We parked in strange little nooks, and John would open the hood of my Nissan 280 ZX and remove a few key parts, making the car impossible to steal. It still had

British Columbia plates on it from Canada, so the parking police cut us some slack, figuring we must be tourists.

As for life in Topanga, our first days were tentative and shy. The one thing we had in common was meditation. John had been a Buddhist for years before becoming a Rastafarian, and was adept at slipping into inner silence.

I had stumbled along with a sort of hit and miss technique, not sure what I was doing, but wanting desperately to make my mind shut up! It was like an answering machine that just kept repeating the same messages over and over and over again! No matter how many times I hit "Stop" and "Erase", it would remind me of the same thing again. John helped me become still. We would sit together in silence in our little room, and realize that deep down, we were the same.

John was still reverberating from the trauma of being homeless, and never completely let his guard down around me. I was ignorantly unaware of what he was going through. In my logical mind, he was off the street, problem solved. John, however, had dealt with so many game players with hidden agendas that he still wasn't sure what I was up to. It was hard for him to imagine that I cared about him, no strings attached.

One day the tension got to me and I decided to get it out in the open. This was how I handled things growing up with a brother who was six foot six. Nothing like a good old knockdown, drag 'em out fight to clear the air and blow the carbon off my valves. I started ranting and raving at John, totally swept away by my rhetoric. When I was done (I didn't notice I was the only one fighting), I went for a walk to cool down. When I came back to our room he was gone. All my relationship training had been with large, angry men. I hadn't dealt with a gentle artist before. My tirade drove him back to the beach.

A day alone in the canyon gave me plenty of time to think about what I'd just put him through. I replayed the fight over and over in my head, becoming more and more embarrassed by my behavior with every rewind. By nightfall I was desperate and drove down to Venice Beach looking for him.

I wasn't on the abandoned boardwalk long before I saw him sitting alone on a log in the dark. Perched next to him was an owl; a small, gray, fluffy, mystical looking owl. I had never seen an owl on that beach before, but there it was keeping him company. Seeing John back on the beach made my heart ache. I had become one more person who had driven him to the street. His feathered sentinel tracked my approach.

I quietly sat next to him on the log. He watched me with world weary eyes. I told him how sorry I was, how I had learned to fight to survive my brother growing up, and I knew I had to change. Finally, to my immense relief, he agreed to come home. My first step in the yoga practice of harmlessness began that night.

*****

One day I stayed at home writing while John canvassed the neighborhood looking for ways to make money. He nicknamed himself "Mr. Five & Dime" because he could solve most people's problems for very little money. He painted signs for local business, detailed cars, cleaned homes. And the philosophical conversation was free. Most people wanted to hang around him while he worked because, like me, they had never met anyone quite like him.

A producer was interested in my children's screenplay, *A Faerie Rade,* and I wanted to go over the script one more time checking for flaws that might ruin the deal. There were a lot of mythical creatures in the script, and the producer wanted a famous Italian "Monster Maker" involved in the project. Being incredibly wary of producers and their reputation for ripping off writers, I said I wanted to meet him.

"No one gets to meet him! He's famous! He's a recluse!"

I didn't care, and I had nothing to lose. I think the producer realized I didn't believe he knew the man. Begrudgingly he drove me out to the bland, concrete block wasteland known as Van Nuys. I was practically blindfolded and spun around ten times to keep me from knowing where we were. I had to promise I would NEVER tell ANYONE where we went. Fine. We went inside a large, non-descript warehouse.

A gentle, humble Italian gentleman politely shook my hand. He was lovely. My script had been translated into Italian for him, and he loved it. While the producer huddled in the background talking on his phone, I was shown around the special effects studio. When we were out of earshot of the producer, the Italian told me an insider secret, "Don't ever give up the rights to your creatures. Mine have financed everything I've done."

I looked over at the producer. He hadn't heard. What a relief to see that there were gracious, artistic human beings in this business.

And now, back in Topanga, I was pouring over the script like it was the Dead Sea Scrolls, trying to make it perfect so I could get a development deal.

Mid morning I heard a tentative knock at the front door of our boarding house. I peeked out of my room and down the hall.

Two ladies stepped into the common living room. "Hello?"

I walked down the hall to greet them; thinking they were looking for one of the other tenants. "Are you the lady who's been rescuing pets?" they asked.

I was. I had been rescuing animals that were being abandoned on our road. It was alarming how many people would simply get bored with a pet and drop it off in Topanga Canyon, confident some kind hearted soul would take care of it. Sadly, most of these animals were immediately run over by some coked up high roller. I had been trying to snatch the puppies and kittens off the road before they became road kill.

The ladies who appeared at my door asked if I would adopt a small kitten they had rescued from coyotes. I hadn't kept any of my rescues; I was simply finding homes for them. I wasn't sure John and I were ready for the commitment of a cat. I knew that in some relationships it could be a deal breaker. But I missed not having a cat as a writing muse. I agreed to at least look at it.

They drove me up the canyon, the muted sun of fall filtering through the towering Eucalyptus trees. As we pulled into the sandy driveway of their quaint little cabin in the hills, I saw cats roaming everywhere. Fur of every hue was rubbed onto my legs in greeting as I stepped out of the car into a feline sea.

I entered the cozy rainbow colored hippie living room and a small grey hairball immediately started hopping around like a windup toy, hissing and spitting at me. I have owned cats my whole life and have to say this was the ugliest thing I had ever seen.

She was so scared her eyes looked like fake plastic appliqués that had been stuck on her head with crazy glue. Her belly was bloated to exploding, her tiny legs and a tail sticking straight out at wild angles. She looked like a surgical glove that had been inflated, a puffer fish with fur. As she backed into a corner, bouncing and spitting, I started to back out the door.

"This isn't going to work."

"Please! Just try taking her for a few days. If she doesn't calm down, bring her back. But we're desperate; our cats are ready to kill her!"

Sure enough, cats perched on high ledges all over the room were figuring out the fastest way to annihilate this badly behaved intruder. The ladies explained that they had heard the kitten crying up in the hills for days, calling for its dead mother. The entire litter had been eaten by coyotes. Somehow she had saved herself by hiding in a thorn bush and eating bugs. She was only a few weeks old, much too young to be weaned. They got me with that story. She was a homie. I reluctantly agreed.

We used a broom to sweep the kitten into a box and took it out to the car. I dreaded thinking what John's reaction would be. I wasn't comfortable making decisions for "Us" yet, and I hoped I hadn't crossed the invisible relationship line too soon.

They drove me back down to the boarding house while the box on the seat next to me bounced maniacally from the kitten hurling itself around inside like a cartoon Tasmanian Devil.

Safely back in our room, I flipped open the lid with a stick and stood back. The dervish flew out. Spellbound, I watched her demolish our nest. She spun around, knocking books off shelves, John's papers off his drawing board, crashing into every possible surface until she skidded to a halt and hid in one of my suitcases. John was gonna love this.

I filled a box full of sand for her to use as a litter, put out some water and tinned cat food, and waited. When John walked in that night, he listened calmly to my story, then lifted the lid of the suitcase and looked in at our new family member.

She was exhausted. Instead of giving him her hip-hop routine, she tried to push herself further into the corner and hide. He pondered the fur ball for a minute. I held my breath.

"She's grey, that's deep."

Exhausted from everyone's 'runnins', we went to sleep. Sometime during the night our new homie joined us. The room was frigid at night with no heat and no insulation in the rickety walls. She must have curled up next to my neck for warmth. Unfortunately, when I attempted to shift position, it startled her awake. She found herself face to face with coyote colored hair. She threw herself at my face and grabbed on with all four sets of needle sharp kitty claws.

I woke up screaming, the rat-cat attached to my face. I became Sigourney Weaver in *Aliens*. I tore the rat-cat off, and threw her across the room. In retaliation, she stomped into the litter box and let loose. It smelt like something had crawled up inside her and died. I opened the window, lit some incense and cursed under my breath.

John mumbled sleepily, "If you two ain't a trip. She's probably full of worms."

The next morning John bought a fresh clove of garlic and a can of tuna from the store downstairs. He carefully chopped up the garlic and buried each small piece in tuna. Slowly, patiently, he fed her one small bit at a time. She wolfed it down hungrily, all the while keeping one eye on me. We had become 'good cop, bad cop'. I was the bad one.

Once she was full we sat back and waited. She made another visit to the litter and this time we had to flee the building. When the fumes had dissipated I cleaned up the worm strewn litter box. Her bloated stomach finally returned to a normal size. What was left was a small rat-like creature, grey spiky fur sticking out in all directions; still not a cat.

That night after dinner, I filled up our little plastic washbasin with hot soapy water to do the dishes. Rat-cat got up on the edge and did a little tight rope walk around the bubbles. John shook his head. "Oh, you bad."

The kitten gave him a smug look of superiority, lost her balance, and fell in. I pulled her out as quickly as I could and wrapped her in a towel. She was so shocked she let me hold her for the first time.

"What should we call her?" I don't know why I asked, I was pretty sure she would be going out with the morning trash. Just then Paul Simon's song "*Gumboots*" came on our tiny cassette player: "... *breakdowns come, and breakdowns go.*"

We looked at each other and laughed, "Breakdown!"

That night, we all slept in peace. The kitten, now known as "Breakdown", coat shiny and smooth from her first bath, curled up peacefully at the end of the bed. I guess that officially made us a family. John found it symbolic that a grey kitten had found its way to us - a blending of our skin colors. "Jah be trippin'."

*****

A story editor in the Hollywood Hills decided to help me rewrite a historical docudrama I had written about the Klondike Gold Rush called *Gold Dust*. On weekdays I'd drop John at Venice Beach then drive up Sunset Boulevard to the Hollywood Hills. It was a bit surreal, sleeping on the floor in Topanga, and spending days with a woman who had a beautiful home, knew all the right people, and complained about life constantly.

Listening to her stories about the good old days typified how disposable people were in the movie business. Once you were discarded, you would do anything to get back to the exclusive inner circle of celebrity.

After a day of wrestling my script into shape I'd pick up John at the beach and head home. Once in the front door and through our communal living room, we'd walk down the hallway to our door. As soon as we opened our door, Breakdown would shoot through our legs and run as fast as she could down the hall. With a flying leap she'd land in the living room and do a victory lap. We'd give her a big cheer, and she would sashay back to the room like the Diva she was. We decided she'd outgrown "Breakdown", and started calling her "Home Run".

Fall turned into winter and our lone little room looked darker, even more barren, emphasizing our lack of "stuff". We decided we deserved a Christmas tree. There was a small convenience store across the street from the health food store that was open late at night. Whenever we had treat money, we'd go there to buy John's favorite candy corns.

But this was no ordinary stroll to the store. We were located at a curve in the road, and at night, with no streetlights, we couldn't see oncoming traffic until it was on top of us. Speed demons from L.A. regularly raced up Topanga Canyon Boulevard at night. Crossing the street in the pitch black meant standing, listening, then sprinting across the street, sort of like playing chicken at the Indie 500 blindfolded.

The convenience store had tiny potted Christmas trees for the holidays. We splurged and bought a $4.99 tree, with a $1.99 string of little lights.

I was getting Christmas cards from friends in Canada, something that amazed John. He had lost touch with everyone he had ever known. I explained to him that in Alberta it was thirty below and everyone was trapped inside. Christmas cards were a way to survive the isolation. In my case, friends waited every year to get a card from me as proof that my latest adventure hadn't killed me. As soon as they had received the cards I'd sent with my General Delivery, Topanga Canyon address, they blasted off their own in reply.

I strung the cards up along the wall. Most of them came in gold foil lined envelopes. I cut the foil into stars and hung these on the tree along with the mini lights. We put the tiny tree in our lone window overlooking the canyon. Many years later I met a woman who said she saw that tree floating in the night sky, and thought it was a vision. She never knew it belonged to two homies and a crazy cat.

*****

Those months in the canyon strengthened our relationship in subtle, unexpected ways. Our nights together were quiet, simple, and nurtured the soul. Home Run provided hours of entertainment. When I washed my hair John would braid it into dozens of tiny braids. It took him several hours. I had never met a man willing to do anything that labor intensive for me. We would listen to our favorite radio programs, usually *The Shadow* and *Larry King*. I had forgotten the art of simply listening and letting the mind create the pictures.

All of this new inner peace was tested one Thursday morning. I was a nervous wreck preparing for the final meeting with a producer interested in my *Faerie Rade* script. I was being given an option agreement to sign. I had dealt with these before, but this one was so convoluted it was almost impossible to understand.

I called a friend of mine who had made it as a blockbuster producer. Her company didn't handle the type of scripts I wrote, but she offered to get me some legal advice. She called her lawyer to see if he was willing to defer his fee until the script sold. She gave me his number and I phoned. He told me he didn't handle small people like me, but as a favor to her, he was willing to look it over for me. At $350 an hour, this was immense. He told me to drop it off at his Century City Office. Too embarrassed to meet him given the sad state of my wardrobe, I decided I'd pretend I was a courier. I'd just nonchalantly drop off the script then go write at the beach. Feeling confident about my plan, I dressed in a halter top and shorts.

After getting lost in Century City for awhile, I finally found the massive glass building. I parked at the curb, hurried inside, through the lobby to the bank of elevators. A security guard had to chase after me and get me to sign in. I forgot I was back in the land of paranoia.

When I finally reached the top floor, the elevator doors swooshed open. It was like stepping onto the bridge of the *Starship Enterprise*. I walked into a massive mahogany and brass waiting room. The sophisticated British secretary at the desk looked up at me over her designer glasses as I stumbled through the plushness of it all. Arriving at her desk, I handed over the envelope.

As I turned to flee, I was stopped by her bright, inquisitive voice. "And are YOU Miss Bishop?"

Damn it! I hate it when people do that.

"Yes?" I wasn't appropriately dressed to say 'yes'.

"One moment, I'll see if he's in."

I panicked. This wasn't the plan. I began sweating in the expensively chilled waiting room, wishing they would just...let...me...leave!

"He'll be right out, have a seat." She gestured to the leather couch under the subtly lit wall art. "Would you like something to drink? Perrier? Grapefruit juice? Espresso?"

My stomach was performing such creative acrobatics, I was afraid that a load of super charged caffeine might result in the meeting being held in the bathroom. I opted for the French tap water.

Now, let me tell you, there is no correct way to sit on a leather couch in shorts. No matter what I did, the lovely sound of thigh suctioning onto hide could be heard. Why did I dress for the beach? Am I a moron?

She handed me the daily trades to read and swooshed back to her desk. From time to time she glanced over and smiled. Suddenly it dawned on me; she was bored out of her ever-loving "long live the Queen" mind. I was probably the first human she'd seen all day. I relaxed. I had done enough temping as a receptionist to know how she felt. I struck up a conversation. When she realized I was a fellow member of the Commonwealth, we were bosom buddies by the time the lawyer appeared in the doorway.

"Miss Bishop?"

I nodded and obediently followed the *Armani* suit into its gilded cage. And it was a cage. Sure, it was a corner office, signifying rank, but he was simply talent in a box. He looked at the contract, then at me.

"I make $350 an hour, but I'm stuck here, and you're heading to the beach, aren't you?"

I grinned sheepishly.

He shook his head at the sad state of his life. "When do you need this by?"

I told him about the Thursday meeting.

"And your number is...?"

"I don't have a phone; just tell me when to call you."

He paused, a slow smile spreading across his face. "Normally I get a number so I can have my receptionist call you and delay a few times just to jerk you around. But apparently, all the balls are in your court."

I liked it. He told me to call Thursday morning early. We shook hands, and I left. I waved at my new friend the receptionist, and made a hasty exit to the elevators. I was freezing!

Thursday morning I hustled downstairs to the pay phone on Topanga Canyon Boulevard and called the lawyer's office. My New Best Friend the receptionist didn't keep me waiting and put my call right through.

The lawyer got straight to the point. "To the casual eye, the contract appears to be correct, but he has made subtle changes which will basically rob you blind."

He carefully explained which clauses had to be edited, and outlined the procedure for calculating my fee, based on the budget of the film. This was the first time insider secrets were being revealed to me. I was ecstatic.

I stood there on the side of the road, the contract balanced on one raised knee while I frantically jotted down his recommendations. He wished me luck, and I hung up the phone. I was going to need more than luck. The idea of facing the producer alone, and pointing out the flaws in his contract, made me feel like I was nine on my way to the principal's office.

Back upstairs in our room John watched me try on every piece of clothing I owned, drop my notes and repeatedly trip over the cat.

"Maybe we should be calling you Breakdown." John picked up my papers and handed them back to me. "Ain't you a trip. This is what you wanted, might as well enjoy yourself."

He was right. I got myself together, gave him a hug and roared down the Pacific Coast Highway to Marina Del Ray. A few hours later I was in a boardroom, across from the producer, systematically correcting his contract. I was enjoying myself, feeling confident, empowered with new knowledge, until I noticed he was getting redder, and redder. I pointed out that he had offered me $1 for a one year option, instead of the standard 10% of the final sale price. Then I explained that I was retaining the rights to the creatures, and the two sequels, until I saw how it was to work with him.

I must have set off some sort of Bubble Bursting Bomb, destroying his dream of ripping off an ignorant writer while he laughed all the way to the bank. “I suppose you have a better offer?”

Yeah, I could go home and stick pins in my eyes. “My legal counsel has advised me against signing this without these revisions.”

“Legal Counsel? You should be grateful I’m even offering you an option! You’re nobody. You’ll never work in this town with your attitude!

He had no idea he was talking to someone who had endured moronic tyrants her whole working life. If I was going to sell a piece I had sweated over for years, I wanted the buyer to be someone with integrity.

Better to die with the world’s greatest collection of unproduced scripts under my bed than regret signing a bogus deal. Right now, I had nothing to lose, no mortgage, no bills. I was free, and my work belonged to me. I smiled my polite Canadian smile, thanked him for his time, and left.

When I got home John could see I needed some comfort food. He knew the pain of having creativity stolen. He fired up the electric wok heated some oil, then added shredded potatoes, carrots, onion and cabbage. Finally he added spices.

"All of life is art, even cooking. People only think they're poor because their food is bland. When you add spice, you're wealthy."

Reveling in our wealth, we sat on the floor and dined.

*****

Two Rastafarian ladies lived across the hall from us. Dreadlocks being a universal language, they were soon John's new best friends. They had a lot in common, notably reggae music and juice bars. The ladies were connected to a group further south in San Diego North County that promoted reggae concerts, cooked for Health Food Stores, and now wanted to build a juice bar. They were looking for someone with experience to pull it off. When they found out about John's years of experience working and renovating juice bars in Los Angeles, a new partnership was formed.

It meant we would move to a town called Leucadia, which is Greek for "Safe Harbor". Apparently this was another town of rebels who, refusing to acknowledge they were sitting in America, referenced Greek Mythology to name their streets. We had never heard of it, but Los Angeles was wearing thin.

The editor I was working with on my Gold Rush project, *Gold Dust,* had taken my finished script to all the wrong producers. The piece was a docudrama, and she kept submitting it to production companies that handled horror and comedies, because they were run by friends. She was inevitably shocked when they turned it down. I reminded her that they didn't handle that genre.

Maybe we should submit it to companies who were actually looking for historical action adventures.

She would just babble incomprehensively; "they owe me", "that doesn't matter", "this was my ticket". Was everyone in this town insane? Or was I just attracting the Fruit Loops? If a woman who had worked in the heart of the movie studios couldn't navigate the development waters, who could?

The idea of distancing myself from this bedlam appealed to me. I could always commute to L.A. if a deal raised its elusive head. We decided to go for it. We left the grid lock and three pack a day air of Babylon in search of Zion.

My two-seater Nissan was too small for the stuff we had accumulated, so our neighbors lent us their big old boat of a Rambler for the move. When the last of John's art supplies were safely stored, we plopped our teenage kitten on top of the beach blankets between us in the front bench seat. She had graduated from Home Run to *The Heathen*, after the famous Bob Marley song. She tucked her paws primly under her chin and stared out the front window, ready for adventure.

John eased the car out of the tall grass. The Rastafarian ladies waved at us as we slid into the traffic on the boulevard. John gently braked for the first of many switch backs. The car merely laughed at us, we had no brakes. Why should the car have brakes? My life didn't at this point, the car was simply following suit. We took corner after corner at warp speed. John quickly dragged a Buddhist chant out of his archive files and started chanting.

We "Om Namyohorengekyo-ed" our way past the pine trees, coyotes, and tourists toward the ocean and the intersection of Topanga and the Pacific Coast Highway. In the distance we could see the light was red. We chanted louder, The Heathen purred happily. Just as we reached the intersection the light turned green and we squealed onto the highway headed south. We didn't stop once all the way to San Diego North County.

15

A NEW SOUL ARRIVES

It was the summer solstice of 1991 and I was sweating bullets in our tiny beach shack near Leucadia Beach. I was in labor. I had only found out four months earlier that I was pregnant. I know, so much for the science degree, but I can explain! I first realized I was pregnant in the fall. But then I miscarried. I didn't think I was pregnant anymore, but it turns out I had miscarried a twin. There was still one in the oven.

When my stomach finally puffed out at Christmas time, John stewed me some prunes, figuring I had just had too much Christmas turkey. Nope. Tummy got bigger. Slowly it dawned on us our family was expanding, and not with more cats. We had gotten married on Earth Day in 1989, and this was the next logical step.

We both had immense fear and distrust of hospitals, so it wasn't hard to convince John to let me deliver at home. My own birth had been a gong show. I was born prematurely with the umbilical cord around my neck. Several 'specialists' tried to remove me from the womb with forceps. After a six hour tug of war, I finally arrived. My hair was jet black, my skin dark purple. They put me in an incubator and showed me to my dad who took one look and said, "That's not mine". No way could this runt belong to his blond haired blue eyed family.

For years after that I was in and out of the hospital for mysterious ailments which the medical professionals never cured. Eventually I healed myself using alternative methods. I learned that most hospitals were not places of healing and I vowed to stay out of them. I figured I couldn't do any worse delivering a baby on my own. Odds were I could do better. And the more I meditated on it, the clearer the message became.

I had been working at a metaphysical bookstore down the back alley from our home. For a writer who was also a spiritual seeker, this was my dream job. John was working as a handyman during the day. Once again, "Mr. Five and Dime" was in business. As we settled in to our new life, he finally began painting again. I had experience selling art back in Canada, so kicked into gear and became his rep. We had people lined up to get one of his $1500 personalized meditation mandalas. The future was so bright, we had to wear shades.

Every morning my 'rush hour' simply involved giving John and The Heathen a kiss and walking down the back alley to the bookstore. Miss Kitty, the store's cat, was always waiting patiently for me on the back step. She was a hefty tuxedo cat who had shown up years ago and adopted the place. I would put the tea on the for customers and psychics who would be arriving, fire up some incense, feed Miss Kitty and tell her how beautiful she was. Then I would have a blissful day chatting with people about all things spiritual.

This was where my real spiritual schooling began. Back in Canada spiritual books were practically contraband they were so hard to find. Only Shirley Maclean's books made it onto bookstore shelves. Here I was exposed to teachings from masters all over the world, and many New Age writers from California. One day as I was putting away some of the used books, one fell off a high shelf and hit me on the head. I reprimanded it and put it back. Next day the book was left on the counter by someone.

Again I put it back. Finally, it hit me on the head again so I read it.

This was how I first learned about the immortal Mahavatar Babaji, from the ancient Vedic tradition in India. He attained enlightenment as a teenager, and has been documented for thousands of years, appearing to people when they were ready for enlightenment. He is considered to be one of the immortals helping mankind. Little did I realize this new knowledge would set a course in my GPS that would shift reality as I knew it.

Meanwhile, when I realized I was pregnant I read every book I could get my hands on about natural birthing: *Spiritual Midwifery, Birth Without Violence, Birth Reborn,* and a little Jane Fonda pregnancy yoga for good measure. That, combined with my science degree and years of training for sports competitions, had given me the tools I felt I needed to do this alone.

As for John, he waited for a sign from Existence that delivering the baby on our own was the right thing to do. After days of indecision, he said to me, "I dreamt it. We can do this." This was how all of his art came to him.

I went into labor at midnight on June 21st, the summer solstice, and slowly, gently, the contractions kept building. I had a beautiful picture on the wall next to the bed that I meditated on. It was a copy of a Tibetan Temple Painting. The scene was of a small pagoda in a garden, protected by enlightened masters sitting on clouds above it. I pictured us being in that pagoda, protected by great souls. It got me through the first eight hours of contractions before I finally woke John up.

John had rigged our tiny studio cabin with every contraption known to man for birthing. A strap was suspended from the ceiling beam so I could hang by my arm pits and take the strain off my hips. We had a birthing chair, water bed, a futon and the floor was covered with a tarp. By the afternoon we had a recording of Dolphin song accompanied by drumming playing in the background. I couldn't get any more California than this. We were ready.

I had increased my meditation practice with the help of one of the psychics from the bookstore. She had home birthed both her sons, and told me being in labor was like surfing, you could ride the wave, or get pulled under by it. She said meditation would help me ride it.

There was also a woman from Ireland at the store during that time. Her name was Mary Malone. She was a world renowned healer and psychic. She and her husband Malcolm, King of the Gypsies, had been traveling around the world for years. She would make money doing psychic readings in wealthy regions, like California, then go to war torn countries to give free healings. She had been awarded a million mile traveler certificate by British Airways for being a world class nomad.

Having her in the bookstore was like having an angel present with a flock of faeries hidden in her blond curls. Whenever she came to town, she would pay me to do secretarial work for her, handle her correspondence, and make arrangements for the next stop on her world tour.

When she found out I was pregnant she gave me the most unique baby gifts imaginable. First, she gave me a free healing. I had suffered a back injury when I was twenty that landed me in the hospital unable to walk or eat. I suffered for years with this, and became known to everyone as "Megan-with-the-bad-back". Bad backs and pregnancy can be a deadly combination. As I put on weight with the baby, I worried that my back would go out and put me back in the hospital. Until Mary came along.

I remember that day in the bookstore. She stood behind me and held her hands a few inches from my back, never touching me. Intense heat shot up my spine and I was told, in my head, by that voice, "This is no longer part of your personality". And just like that, my back was healed.

Next she gave me a free reading. We sat in a small reading room, illuminated only by candlelight. She had me pour water into a glass, then she stared intently into it. She saw an olive skinned woman wearing a tam holding the child. The person she described was John's mother, who had passed away many years before. The message was simple, the birth was blessed. That was the final green light from the universe that I needed.

By now our small beach shack had John's original artwork hanging everywhere. Our small garden off the porch was full of easels holding massive oil paintings. He loved doing abstracts. To be honest, I didn't understand most of what he painted. That all changed when I went into labor. I saw the paintings from an altered state, and stunning images began appearing from the swirls of color on the canvas. Excitedly I told John what I was seeing.

"You mean you had to be in labor to see what I paint?" I could feel his sadness. It was the story of his life, being inspired to paint what others could never see.

As the day wore on, I began to have my doubts about pulling this off. I meditated, we did "Chi" breathing, we chanted, we were exhausted. By late afternoon John became philosophical about the holding pattern we found ourselves in.

"So, if you decide not to let this baby come out, will it reabsorb into your body?"

"Shut up."

"You know elephants are pregnant for TWO years!"

"Shut...up!"

The Heathen was delighted by all of this. She had delivered her litter the year before and let me witness it. I remembered her moving quietly around the cardboard box I had prepared for her, purring and licking each kitten baggie that exited her body. She never stayed still; she kept moving and shifting, helping the babies exit. I followed her lead; constantly moving to different places in the room, easing the pressure off my spine as the baby moved along the birth canal.

To celebrate this momentous occasion, The Heathen brought me gifts - live butterflies, moths, bugs of all descriptions. At one point, I was panting in the birthing chair when she flew through the window and let a huge moth loose at my feet. As it shot towards my face I snatched it out of the air and shoved it at John.

"Take it outside."

Maybe it was the deep, male *Exorcist* voice coming out of me that freaked him out, but John got the message. He hustled The Heathen and the moth outside for their own safety. A few more breaths and I slid into a deep trance and for the first time, I consciously exited my body.

I found myself standing in front of a golden wall of hieroglyphs, and the Voice that had guided me all these years joined me. I realized I was in the presence of the Divine, and my real birthing coach.

"I don't think I can do this," I whispered.

"You are not being harmed; you are just driving this vehicle".

I saw myself stepping into my body, the way I got into my car. I understood. My body was a tool for me to use, nothing more, and it was now on auto pilot. It knew what to do, as long as I didn't interfere and screw things up with my fear.

"Why isn't this baby coming out?"

"Because you refuse to stop being a child. This baby needs you to be a mother."

I pouted for a minute before I realized it was right. I had bopped along, dodging responsibility, for a long time. John and I were like two kids. Someone had to step up and be the adult. I promised I would.

"Please let this baby be born," I whimpered.

"Don't be a beggar!" roared the Voice, "Demand it as a child of God!"

"I DEMAND this baby be born!" I roared to the Cosmos.

While this drama was exploding in my inner space, outside John sat across from me, trying not to fall asleep in the intense summer heat. While I was roaring inside my soul, he said externally I wasn't making a sound. In fact, he had to poke me with a stick from time to time, to make sure I was still alive. He didn't want to get too close in case that male *Exorcist* voice returned.

I was leaning forward on a chair when I finally resurfaced and whispered to him, "Can't you see anything?"

John put on his reading glasses and checked my, er, nether regions. He shook his head. "All I see is a membrane or something."

"It can't be a membrane, my water broke hours ago!"

Words failing him, John got a pencil and pad of paper, and began sketching what he was seeing. He drew a circle and scribbled wildly until it was all cross hatching. Great, it was indecipherable. He peered closer, I felt a 'pop' and John said, "This is it!"

The baby had crowned. What he had been looking at wasn't membrane but a head full of black hair. He had been looking for a bald baby. He got to work lubricating the opening with Almond Oil to prevent my skin from tearing. Suddenly, there was another contraction and John found himself face to face with what he could only describe as *Frankenstein;* a square purple face with long black hair.

John instinctively jumped back, then his brain reminded him he was going the wrong way, and he moved in closer. That's when he saw the cord around the baby's neck. We had practiced for this. Many experts have found women repeat their birth trauma. When I warned John the baby could have the cord around its neck, he practiced on himself using one of his drum ropes. He realized it had to be lifted forward, toward the navel. Doing it the other way double looped the rope, which is what I believe the 'experts' did to me.

All his practice paid off. He quickly slid the umbilical cord over the baby's head towards the navel, then sat back on his haunches, prepared to wait some more. There was another massive contraction, and at five in the afternoon, our son came flying into the world, literally. All my muscles bore down on the child, and he flew towards John, umbilical cord unraveling behind him. Good thing John had good hands, because he caught him like a football in midair.

I had been in an extremely altered state during labor, and felt an energy hovering behind me until the tiny body appeared. As soon as John caught him, I felt a rush as a spirit flew over my shoulder and into the compressed, purple piece of flesh. It entered the body and caused it to open like a flower, turning pink with the first breath.

John had threatened to hold the baby by its feet and smack its butt, the way they do on TV. I told him as long as the umbilical cord was attached it would pump air into the baby. It was a safety net until the lungs began working. There was no need to rush or smack anyone!

John wasn't convinced. "I'm all alone with you. If I don't hear a sound out of that kid, I'm smacking it!"

The kid got the message and turned to John and squawked like a duck. John and I looked at each other in amazement, then burst out laughing.

"Get the tub!" I ordered.

Adrenalin kicked in and the hypnotic monotony of the afternoon disappeared. We had work to do. I laid the baby face down on my chest to help clear the breathing passages. John hustled into the bathroom to fill up a baby bath. I checked the time, knowing the astrologers at the store would want to know. Suddenly John's head popped out of the bathroom.

"What is it?"

In all our excitement, we hadn't checked. I peeked.

"It's a boy!"

We put him in a small baby bath full of warm water. I had read that water helps lessen the shock of gravity for a newborn. Beautiful afternoon sunlight filtered into the cabin through the trees, and our son opened his eyes, gazing around at us, pushing himself away from the edges of the tub with his tiny hands.

The extent of the baby's awareness shocked us both, but I had read that natural birth doesn't drug the baby, and you should expect them to be aware.

"Baby's should be born into the same atmosphere in which they are conceived," says Michael Odent, who wrote *Birth Reborn.* Our son was born in the room he was conceived in, surrounded by an ethereal garden.

"What should we call him?" whispered John.

The image of the Poet on Venice Beach floated into my head. We had never seen his name written down, but I had heard it, so I made up my own spelling.

"Esah", I smiled.

John started to cry.

As we were in no rush to cut the cord, we completely forgot about the final step, delivery of the placenta. It was something that is written about quite seriously, about "delivering" the placenta, and how women have bled to death because of doctor's tugging on the cord trying to detach it. My placenta got tired of waiting and shot out across the floor on its own while we played with our new baby.

Once we were sure Esah was breathing well on his own, John tied off the umbilical cord about one inch from the baby's belly, then used some sterilized wire cutters to cut it. Then he took the placenta and cord into my garden and buried them. Finally, he cleaned everything up and made me a huge fish dinner.

My parents had finally accepted the fact that I had married a homeless black artist; so I figured they could handle anything now. I picked up the phone and dialed Canada. After a few pleasantries I told them I was at home, holding their new grandson in my arms. No, a doctor hadn't been present.

"But what about the cord?" My mother was frantic. She was terrified my baby had undergone the same strangulation I had.

"It was around his neck. John flicked it off with his finger."

There was silence at the other end of the line, then a very controlled, angry voice spoke. "Three specialists choked you for six hours, and an artist flicked it off with his finger?"

I could see her getting ready to launch a law suit. After many congratulations, my parents hung up and proceeded to pour themselves some stiff drinks. We turned off the phone, locked the door, and went to bed.

Thc next morning I called the bookstore and gave them the news. The psychics there had a betting pool going regarding the day of the birth and the sex of our baby. Funny, I would have thought they would all be right. But the bets were all over the map. As each guess was crossed off the chart, only one remained; the summer solstice.

John was looking out the kitchen window when the baby pool winner appeared. "There's a big, angry looking woman heading our way."

The woman was a German psychic. She was a loner who lived with a pack of wolves. She had found the orphaned litter next to their dead mother, so brought them home and raised them. She was definitely a unique individual. She told me once she had trouble looking directly at people because their information scrolled above their heads like a stock market ticker tape.

And apparently, she had won the baby pool. She didn't bother to knock, just stormed into our tiny cabin and tossed a fistful of money at the bed. I lay there, holding our child, money raining down on our heads.

"You won!" I giggled. "But this is your money!"

"I didn't want the money. I just wanted to be right!"

She told me that she had had a vision of me walking down the street holding the hand of a small boy. She gave me a smug grin behind her dark sunglasses and left. And the woman who lived with wolves became the first in a long line of visitors. The whole town lit up with the news. Some of the men in our neighborhood took John aside and interrogated him about the birth.

"Man, weren't you grossed out by it?"

"I've held so many dying homies in my arms," was John's soft reply, "to hold a new life was a blessing."

"But didn't the mess make you sick?" asked another.

John shook his head. "Man, I did so much acid in the sixties; I was just trippin' on the colors."

As we lay in bed that night, unable to stop staring at our child, the Heathen curled up by our feet purring.

Suddenly I burst out laughing. “Oh, No!”

“What?”

“My brother’s name is Tom!”

“You’re telling me my son has an Uncle Tom? Jah, what you doing to me?”

I hugged him and thanked him for letting me do something no other man would have let me attempt.

“That’s it,” he replied, “I’m hanging up my spurs, and closing the gate behind me. I’ve seen it all.

16

INSIDE THE WALL

Little did I know how prophetic those words would be. As an abused child, John was in danger of being an abusive father. “You become what you hate,” he often told me. And he hated his father. His father tried to beat the artist out of John. Therapists say that the birth of a child, to someone who has been abused, is a make or break situation; they can heal, or sail off the cliff. John sailed.

Maybe it was the fear that he would become his father, or the fear that he wasn’t up to the challenge of supporting a family. I’ll never know. The day after Esah was born John took him out and proudly showed him off to the neighborhood.

The next day he disappeared without a word. We were low on groceries, and after waiting all day for him to return, I realized I had to go. Every inch of my body was sore as I put Esah in the snuggly and shuffled over to our friend’s grocery store on the Pacific Coast Highway.

I hadn’t had a chance to weigh him so loaded I him onto the produce scale. A lady came up behind me and peeked at the little bundle suspended in the air, “Are those on sale?”

Visiting with friends helped lift my spirits, but returning home to our empty shack fueled any post partum depression that was lurking, waiting to spring on my fragile psyche. When John came home he seemed remote, distant, not the man I married.

He was elusive about where he had been, and treated me more like his mother than his wife. He began disappearing more and more. I started having nightmares that he wasn't coming back. Many times he didn't reappear until the next morning.

I finally exploded. A strange smile spread across his face. "I never really believed you loved me until now." That's how he was raised, people who love you yell at you. It wasn't how I was raised, and I could feel myself sinking in confusion.

After two months of maternity leave I returned to the bookstore, Esah riding on my back in his backpack. It was soothing to return to a familiar place, with people who cared about me. I could tell from the guarded looks of the psychics that they knew something was up with John. They offered subtle advice about anti-depressant herbs and supplements. Looking back, I wonder how much of the darkness that was to come was visible to them.

Esah loved coming to work. He rode in his backpack and stared over my shoulder at customers. He took in all the social interactions and reveled in the energy of the crystals that filled the store. By mid morning I would breast feed him in the back office until he fell asleep, then place him on the book cart where I could keep an eye on him.

The neighborhood and resident psychics were always interested in his progress, and were constantly dropping off little presents for us.

I had read that we are all capable of manifesting what we need to live. I had experienced hints of it, but the Manifesting Bureau began working overtime when Esah arrived. When we needed a car seat, two appeared. When I was looking for a stroller, we got three. My friends held a baby shower for us and I told them I'd only accept their used baby clothes, since they all had kids. We ended up with enough clothes to last for years. My friends in Canada contributed to a diaper service for the first few months, and presto! Clean diapers were delivered to the door of our shack every week, and the dirty ones carted away.

I had learned from the healer Mary Malone how important it is to welcome a new soul into this world. Many children brought to her for healing had never been christened, or baptized, or officially welcomed into the family. She said the soul didn't know it was supposed to stay if there wasn't a ceremony. Most ailing children brought to her were healed with a simple family naming ceremony.

I asked two of the psychics from the store if they would do the honors and give Esah a blessing ceremony. One practiced Native American traditions, and John was part Blackfoot, so the women set up a Medicine Wheel in our side garden. We invited our best friends who lived down the alley to join us. One bright sunny morning we all stood in the garden for Esah's welcoming ceremony. John and I stood in the center of the Medicine Wheel, holding the baby, and systematically turned to face each of the four directions, while the women blessed him.

Sometimes, John seemed to be his old self. He'd play with the baby, show him off to friends, fondly nicknaming him "Mr. Penny", you know, the son of "Mr. Five and Dime". He even started a new painting. It was four feet in diameter, shaped like a hexagon - a meditation mandala in honor of his son. When it was finished, the bookstore owner was so impressed she asked John to teach a mandala painting class at night. I hoped it would get us back on track.

But it was already too late. By 1992 we were struggling through Esah's first year, trying to balance our lives, when John's world exploded. A black man, Rodney King, was beaten by police one night in Los Angeles. An onlooker caught it on his video camera. The uproar that followed the trial had America holding its breath, and John glued to the television twenty-four hours a day. At first, I was glad that he was staying home more. But then the verdict came down, the white policemen involved in the beating were "Not Guilty". Riots erupted on the streets of Los Angeles, an eerie replay of the Kansas City riots John had witnessed as an art student. Los Angeles burned, and with it, John's sanity.

As the night wore on, CNN showed scene after scene of riots in the city north of us. John turned and looked at me with all the hate the black community was feeling against whites. I was powerless to stop the transmogrification of my world. By midnight he was gone.

When John's body walked in the door the following day, a cold chill crawled up my spine. I looked into the cold, dark eyes of the creature in front of me. It was something, or someone else. John screamed incomprehensibly, whirled around and grabbed the carving axe he used to make Djembe drums. He headed for Esah's crib.

I blocked his path and grabbed our sleeping child, hoping to get out the door. But he was quicker. He dropped us to the ground, knee on my throat as I clutched Esah. I let out an unearthly roar. It startled both of us and froze John mid swing.

Our dysfunctional surfer neighbors heard me and crashed through the door, thinking something was wrong with the baby. Instead they saw John, eyes crazed, axe held high. They moved fast and pulled him off. But as soon as they let him go he retreated into the night.

They tried to calm me down, saying that wasn't my husband; crack lets other things walk in, and that John would be back. There it was. They said it. John had become what he hated, a Crack addict. Ironic this wisdom coming from guys who had been high for years. Addiction is like to setting your hair on fire and trying to put it out with a hammer. The surfers meant well, but their hair was on fire.

A few nights later the creature that looked like John returned intent on getting into a tug of war with me over Esah. I realized in horror that we were trying to pull our son in two. I let go and John, caught off guard, pulled with such force that he slammed Esah's head into a wall.

The Voice that had been quiet since Esah's birth thundered in my head, "If you do not remove this child from this situation, I will take him away from both of you!"

The Universe had given me this amazing gift, and I was going to lose him. We had to get away from this monster. Slowly, and silently, we disappeared and went underground where John couldn't find us. My soul hid in a dark corner and quietly shut the door.

*****

John emptied our bank account and vanished into a crack house. I became homeless with our son. No more diaper service, food in the fridge, or TV to relax to while Esah napped.

And the man I loved with every ounce of my being was gone. It was my turn to be inside the wall. My brain shut down. It took all of my concentration to keep Esah fed, and the cloth diapers I bought for him washed.

We found places to stay, floors to sleep on, places to house sit, and I managed to keep us from being on the street at night.

Esah had started walking and was a busy toddler so I had to leave the bookstore. I got a job working at a small Topiary Shop on the Pacific Coast Highway, and it became our sanctuary. The owner was looking for a store cat; so I moved The Heathen to the store. Every day Esah and I would walk to the Topiary Shop and spend the day among the plants and our pet.

The store had wire frames of every creature imaginable, and I planted them with ivy and moss to create topiary animals. Esah would take customers by the hand and introduce them to his botanical menagerie. “Bunny, Kitty, Puppy”.

When it was time for his nap, I would put him down on his mat in the small closet like office at the back, and we would post a sign on the door, “Manager at work, do not disturb”. The owner of the store paid me cash at the end of each day, and we kept afloat. Everything I tried to do to get us out of our predicament failed. The degree, the resume, my good intentions amounted to nothing.

I finally understood what Post Traumatic Stress Syndrome felt like. Now I was the war vet. Simple solutions became impossible. I had completely lost my bearings. And John, my anchor for the past three years, was gone. I lay awake at night trying to understand why he was behaving this way. The man I had spent every waking moment with, who I thought I knew inside out, had become a stranger to me. My brain frantically scrambled around trying to find something to cling to, something to keep us from sinking. But there was nothing. Esah and I had no choice but to be still.

My Sunday calls to my parents back home in Canada had become increasingly strained. "Why don't you just come home?" they wailed.

I couldn't. I couldn't travel with my child without written consent from his father. John was nowhere to be found, and when he did show up, paperwork wasn't on his agenda. I got a book out of the library on how to do your own divorce in California. It was the only way I could get custody of Esah and make it back to Canada to see my ailing dad before he died.

"Why don't you put Esah in daycare and get one of those high paying marketing jobs you used to have!" my mom would plead.

That, too, wasn't an option. All my friends had home based businesses. They were barely able to look after their own kids. The few tentative tries I'd made at having strangers take care of Esah had been disastrous. One mom tossed him into a swimming pool, not bothering to ask me if he could swim. He couldn't. I realized the only one who would be taking care of my son was me. And he, in turn, was the only thing keeping me sane.

And then a strange message was given to my mom. She went to a psychic, just for fun. Instead of receiving a fluffy message about winning the lottery, the Psychic told her to stop trying to get me back to Canada.

"She is fulfilling her karma. She has to finish this. If you make her leave now you will do her more harm than you can imagine."

*****

One Sunday Esah was down to his last diaper. The diaper service had ended, and I was using cloth diapers I had bought. I hunted through everything to find enough change to do one load at the Leucadia Laundromat. It was a tiny, one room building on the wild, untamed side of the Pacific Coast Highway. Local surfers and tourists staying at the quaint beach motels would come here to do laundry and sit outside enjoying the California climate.

Using all of our worldly treasure, I got a load of cloth diapers into a washer, and then took Esah outside to play in the undeveloped vacant lot next to the Laundromat. It was nothing but a pile of dirt, weeds, and volunteer flowers, but to a fifteen month old it was a veritable paradise. We wrangled pill bugs, dodged fire ants, built castles out of twigs, anything to keep my mind off our situation.

Back inside I moved the diapers into the giant industrial dryer, almost home free. As long as Esah didn't decided to put the mother lode of pooh into the last clean diaper he had on, we were safe.

The small Laundromat had one long counter along the wall with windows and an island counter for folding clothes. An older gentleman was using the counter by the window. He had the worn look of an alcoholic traveling salesman; burst blood vessels on his large bulbous nose, thinning hair, and a worn suit jacket. He was putting dress shirts on hangers and hanging them on a rod across the back seat of his car that was parked just outside the open door.

I decided to teach Esah some manners and showed him how to shake hands and say "How do you do?"

He giggled and practiced a few times. Then, using all three month's worth of walking skills, lurched around the counter to the older gentleman and stuck out his tiny, pudgy hand. "How D' Do?" he gurgled.

The man grinned shyly and bent down to the thirty inch munchkin in front of him. "How do you do, sir?"

Esah exploded with laughter and rumbled around the centre island back to me. He tripped to a stop and stuck out his hand. "How D' Do?"

I shook his hand, "How do YOU do?"

We played the game until all our clothes were dry. The gentleman nodded at me as he left with his last load. I was finishing folding diapers when he came rushing back into the Laundromat.

His face was flushed; sweat streaming down his forehead. I was afraid he was having a heart attack. He grabbed my hand with both of his. "You're a wonderful mother!" he cried. Then, embarrassed, he bolted out the door.

In my hand he had left a sweaty, rumpled twenty dollar bill. A soft breeze moved the air around me like a caress. God was using other people to get to me. I had to learn to let go, and trust in Existence.

*****

My years of standing on the California fault line came to a head one desolate, rainy night. I was huddled in an abandoned motel room behind the Topiary Shop. Esah was bundled in a shiny silver emergency blanket on top of a pile of boxes. The Heathen crouched on the window sill, looking at me with otherworldly green eyes and flicking her tail. The rain poured in under the door, threatening to flood the room.

I cried until nothing was left. I cried for all I had been, all I thought I'd lost, and the situation I had put my child in. I sat alone in my desolation, and finally surrendered.

I spoke to the night, "God, I give up. I don't know how I got here, and I don't know how to make this stop. Whatever you want me to do for the rest of my life, I'll do it. I surrender."

The Voice in my head was quiet. Maybe it was too late. I didn't realize it at the time, but being cut off from everything I thought would rescue me, was the first step to allowing Existence to show me it was with me all along.

The next morning the rain stopped. It was another perfect California day. An eerie calm settled over me. I said a prayer and meditated. I asked what I should do.

"Call her," was all I got.

The image of one of the playgroup moms floated into my mind. She and her husband were small space gardeners. Their son was a little older than Esah. I went to the pay phone and made put in the last of my coins. I had barely hung up the receiver at the phone booth when her Isuzu screeched to a halt in front me. I think she actually made time go backwards.

"Thank God you finally called!" said my "small space" friend. "This whole town has been waiting for you to ask for help. But you're so proud, we didn't want to insult you, so we've been waiting for you to ask."

I was struck dumb. I wasn't fooling anyone. The whole town knew what was happening to me, I was the only one in denial. Just as "Mom" on Venice Beach was too embarrassed to tell her mother that she was homeless, I was afraid to admit to anyone I needed help. What has happened to our society that we feel we have to be perfect or there is no place for us?

That day, everything changed. Everything I had ever been, or ever learned about living was gone. Esah and I moved in with the small space gardeners. I had money in my pocket from making topiaries, Esah had toys and a friend to play with, we were eating amazing meals, and they wouldn't accept a dime from me. It was hard to completely relax. I was still twitching, waiting for the next emotional tremors to hit.

I remembered how John had been when we first left the beach and moved to Topanga Canyon. Now I was the ex-homie. But it was obvious something inside me had shifted forever.

"When heaven is about to confer a great office upon a man, it first exercises his mind with suffering, and his sinews and bones with toil. It exposes him to poverty and confounds all his undertakings. Then it is seen if he is ready."

~Moshi

The Heathen was staying at the store full time, seemingly happy about being the Topiary mouser. But one night, as Esah and I crossed the Pacific Coast Highway to go home, our beautiful grey cat tried to follow us. I waved my arms and told her to go back to the store. She sat staring at me with those green eyes that had seen so much; from being alone in Topanga Canyon to witnessing the birth of Esah. I prayed she wouldn't follow.

The next morning the sky was full of clouds, an air of foreboding engulfed me as I walked to work. Esah stayed with our friends on a play date, and I was alone with my thoughts. As I crossed the highway, my boss and dear friend came running over to me crying.

"It's The Heathen! She was hit, I found her this morning."

I followed her to the curb in slow motion. She had carefully covered the small body with a cardboard box. I lifted it and saw my old friend. She didn't understand why we didn't take her with us. She wanted so badly to follow us, she had tried to cross the deadly highway. As I gently picked her up and took her out back to bury her, I realized the death of the Heathen also marked the death of my marriage to John. The grey being that had symbolized our union was gone.

As I held her, I felt a light energy absorb back into my body. It was as if she had manifested from me, and had simply returned, much the way we return to the Divine once our journey on this Earth is over. Maybe she knew how hard it would be for Esah and me to find places to live if we had a pet with us, and had gracefully bowed out of the adventure.

It was time for us to carry on alone.

*****

Another single mom in our playgroup had a son Esah's age. One day she asked if I'd like to house sit while she went on vacation. We moved into her place, high on the hill overlooking the ocean, and I knew this was what I wanted for us; a small, cozy armchair of a place to curl up in and create a life.

Unfortunately, it took a lot of false starts before this happened. As I hunted for that perfect homestead for me and my toddler, I realized I wouldn't find it on the strip. The Pacific Coast Highway was so full of drugs, it was impossible to create a normal life there.

For a while I rented a room from a single mother and her two children. She seemed fine at first, but it quickly became obvious that she was an alcoholic and her boyfriend a Crack head. Their favorite Saturday night entertainment was to do their drug of choice then throw glass vases at each other. The grand finale involved me running out of the house with all of our kids in tow and calling the police.

One night, as I delayed going home to the gong show as long as possible, I sat with Esah on the cliffs overlooking the ocean. My answering machine of a mind kept trying to play my options to me over, and over and over again. It would not shut up. I kept hitting the stop button, and tried to watch the sun slipping slowly into the Pacific Ocean, but it kept starting up. It was driving me crazy!

We could see the beach from where we were sitting. I watched all the moms load their kids and beach toys into their SUVs, heading home to have dinner. Maybe it was pizza night and they would rent a movie. That answering machine in my head started telling me what a loser I was. I turned it off and looked at my happy toddler, playing with sticks and bugs in the sand.

“You know, when I was in Canada, I used to spend thousands of dollars to come sit on this coastline and watch the sunsets. Now, I'm doing it for free!”

“For free!” said the little parrot next to me.

That made me feel a little better. For a moment, then the gloom slowly eased in again. I started to cry. I turned away so he couldn't see, and tried to calm down. I felt the light touch of an angel on my arm. “Don't cry, mommy. What's wrong?”

“We need to find a safe home, Sweetie.”

He went back to his playing, and as darkness fell I gathered our things.

"Let's go, Buddy."

He struggled to pick up a huge ball of Torrey Pine needles.

"Oh, don't bring that with you", I pleaded.

He proudly showed me the bird's nest balanced in his hands.

"But look! I found us a home!"

*****

During this time the original John seemed to resurface and one day we were able to have a sane conversation, in public, at the beach. He agreed to go to counseling with me. Because of that, I was able to let him start spending time with Esah again. John would come by the topiary shop, load Esah into the backpack, and go off on his 'runnins'.

He was encouraged that we were talking, and one day started giving me a sales pitch about how we should live together again. I felt sick to my stomach. Not enough had changed for me to risk that kind of danger again. As he went on and on, I became more and more uncomfortable. John looked at me hopefully, "What do you think?"

I remembered something the therapist had told me to say. "I'm not comfortable with that."

We sat in silence for a moment, then a huge smile spread across his face. "What a great answer! I'm not even mad! I have to remember to use that!"

He started doing signs again for local businesses, and I prayed that he would return to that amazing man I loved. I was wrong, again. One day I was at the shop working and he had Esah with him for the day. Out of nowhere he called, "I'm taking Esah back to L.A. We're going underground; you'll never see him again." It's a weird sensation when the right side of your head explodes. Kind of leaves a mess.

I hung up the phone and staggered over to my friend. "Get the car!" roared that *Exorcist* voice of mine. Without a word she grabbed her keys and we ran. I filled her in as fast as I could, but I couldn't really hear what I was saying because my heart was pounding so loudly.

Time moved in slow motion while a vision played in my head. I was reminded of the story of the immortal, Mahavatar Babaji. He was kidnapped as a child and sold into slavery. But it ended up being a blessing. His parents were such strict, religious people, they would have actually hindered his spiritual growth. As it was he was given his freedom by the slave owner, and trained under an enlightened master. He attained enlightenment as a teenager, and appears in that form to any true seeker.

The Voice managed to get my attention through the breakdown happening in my brain, "He doesn't belong to you."

Just as Babaji had to be removed from parents who might stop his development, I was standing at a crossroads. Could I give control of Esah back to God? Or would I cling to him like some crazed control freak? I realized that this could be the end of me. If I didn't learn the lesson being shown to me, I would be one of those women on Venice Beach who had taken a blow and never recovered. This event could put me on the street for good.

I stilled myself and asked what I should do. I was told I didn't own this soul, he belonged to God. I was just his physical guardian. So I made a deal with the Voice. "If you bring him back to me, I promise I'll care for him as long as he needs me. But I understand he's yours. When it's time for him to leave me, I won't stop him."

That was it, lesson over. By the end of the day the police had brought him back to me. I believe with all my heart that if I hadn't come to this realization, Esah would never have returned.

I pondered all of this the next day, holding Esah's hand, walking with my head down staring at my feet. I had been given a second chance to care for this child, but was I up for it? Could I give him what he needed?

"Look up," said the Voice. I dragged my gaze away from the sidewalk and looked up. A huge circle of clouds resembling the upper torsos of people surrounded me. Suddenly I felt like I was a game piece on a giant board game, being moved around the board by these giant beings. And they were laughing at me.

I realized we were like creations in a video game. We'd get up in the morning, step into our bodies/controllers, and confront tasks and challenges that would earn us points. At the end of the day, er, game, it would end. The next day we would start another one. All we have is the present, to play the game the best we can, then turn it off at night.

I vowed to play the game to win, beginning that moment.

17

GREENHOUSES AND FLOWER FIELDS

One of the people hanging around us those days was a musician who had once been a child actor. He was very good looking in a Prozac-induced, surfer kind of way. He knew I was trying to find a place to live off the strip, away from all the drug dealing. One day he offered to rent me a room in his mansion on top of the hill in the greenhouse district.

I wasn't sure this was a good move. Living with him could be just as bad, or worse, than what I was already dealing with. He was a musician, a bachelor, and a bit of a Peter Pan, you know, a boy trapped in a man's body. And I didn't know him that well. He could sense my misgivings so he invited Esah and me to spend a night and try the place out.

I was desperate to change our situation so I agreed. He came and picked us up one day and drove us away from the madness of the strip, and into the Leucadia hills. We drove past Poinsettia ranches and fields of begonias. As we pulled into the driveway I admired the palm tree farm across the street from him.

The topiary shop I worked for had moved off the strip and was just down the road. I would be five minutes from work. And to top it off, it was breathtakingly beautiful, and peaceful.

He showed us a guest room, but Esah and I opted to sleep on the huge balcony that ran the length of the back of the house. We awoke to birds singing as the sunrise peeked at us through the orchard that filled his backyard.

Hmm, such a hard decision, stay here in apparent paradise or go back to the crack infested strip? I accepted The Musician's offer and we moved up the hill.

The bonus was that now I could make topiaries at home. The shop agreed to deliver ivy and frames to the house for me. Esah didn't have to be corralled in a pen to avoid being run over on the Pacific Coast Highway anymore. He was free to charge around the backyard with The Musician's wonderful Dalmatian dog, Cookie. She helped fill the void left by The Heathen's death. I think the dog was happy to have people in the house as well, especially a "mom" who would remember to feed her.

After breakfast every morning Esah and I would go for a walk down the back lane with Cookie, examining bugs, watching butterflies, and visiting the neighbors' dogs. Many of them crawled under their fences to come hang out with us while their owners were away at work.

Esah was two and in the middle of being potty trained, which, as any working mother will tell you, is reason enough not to have more kids. Enduring labor was nothing compared to potty training. One day, after three changes of soiled clothes, I was so frustrated I took all Esah's clothes off. I figured he could squat on the ground if he had to. I needed to get some work done and make us some money. I was still thinking I was somehow in charge of our fate and the one paying the bills. It takes a while to truly surrender to Existence.

As Esah ran around the backyard with Cookie, his blond curls barely visible above the dog's back he looked like some kind of wild animal himself. Bit by bit, the neighborhood dogs crawled under the fence and joined the game until Esah was running with a substantial pack of very happy dogs.

When The Musician and his buddy surfers returned to the house after a morning of riding waves, they were confronted with the sight of my naked child running with the pack. He was immediately nicknamed “Dog Boy of Leucadia”.

“Raised by a pack of wild dogs,” they announced in their best radio announcer voices, “living in the wilds of Leucadia, California.”

And so, Esah became “Dog Boy”.

The Musician rented the other bedroom in the large house to a Vietnam Vet, a massage therapist who had been a Viet Cong interrogator. His room was across the hall from mine, and at night he would speak Viet Cong in his sleep, aggressively interrogating ghost prisoners from the past.

It was a bit unsettling, but as I got to know the quiet, haunted man, we became friends. Over time all of us residents at the house realized we were disasters when it came to choosing mates, so we started creating a dating checklist which had to be filled out before anyone got permission from the other roommates to go on a date.

Week by week, the list got longer and longer, until it would have been impossible for anyone to pass this test: Did you love your mother? Were you breastfed? Are you an alcoholic? Drug addict? Do you hate your father? Do you like kids? Do you have a job? Are you under psychiatric care? (The Musician took offense to this one) Have you done time?

One day the masseuse asked if I would be interested in a trade. He had seen me sewing, and needed some clothes fixed. Meanwhile, I had such bad "stress balls" in my shoulders and neck; I couldn't lift my arms above shoulder height to work on the taller topiaries. A deal was struck. In exchange for mending his clothes, I could get one hour of Shiatsu massage.

I knew this one session might be my only chance to get "fixed" so when he asked how much pressure he could use, I told him to go for it. I lay on the floor while all 6'2" of him stood on my back and dug his heels into my shoulders. As I took long deep breaths, I could finally feel my muscles relaxing.

"These come from having the weight of the world on your shoulders," he explained. "I like working on moms, they know how to breathe through the pain. Men are wimps."

After that session, I was able to work on the tall topiaries again, lifting my arms above my head to pin the ivy on life size giraffe frames, hippos, elephants (for the Republican convention), and Chinese Fu Lions. The back yard started to resemble an enchanted garden with all my ivy creations dotted amongst the fruit trees.

And I started to experience moments of profound peace and clarity. They didn't last long, but they gave me hope. This was the state of being I wanted to exist in, and I started getting rid of the things in my life that disrupted that feeling.

I continued to try to work things out with John, except now, when I went to the beach to visit with him, I had body guards. We'd catch a ride with The Musician or one of the surfers. If John was sane, we'd stay and visit. If it was the creature on crack waiting for us, we'd turn around and leave. Esah could always spot this second John faster than I could. I wondered if he could see the weird energy around him. When we were within twenty feet of John, Esah would turn away if it wasn't safe. Having other males around made John behave.

After one long day of work, the guys took pity on me and suggested I sit down and rest, while they got Esah bathed and put to bed. Relief washed over me, finally, a break. I was overwhelmed with their kindness. I mean, they were nice guys and all, but basically self-centered bachelors with no responsibilities. I think they liked having a "mom" on the premises, someone who constantly cleaned, removed dead mice from the back of the fridge, and remembered to feed the dog.

I took them up on their offer and sat in the rarely used living room. My mind went numb as I watched the sun go down in peace. An old memory popped into my head of a summer in the Okanagan with my family. We had rented a cabin and were enjoying a carefree summer vacation. As we kids roared in and out of the lake, up and down the beach, I noticed Mom sitting, staring out at nothing, a slight trickle of drool escaping from her mouth.

"Mom! You're not having any fun," I yelled as I raced by.

"I'm fine."

"But you're not doing anything!"

She simply smiled a soft, far away smile. I had become that woman. I didn't want to do anything. Just sitting, staring off into space was heaven. I closed my eyes and sighed. Then I felt a light tap on my shoulder. I cracked open one eye.

“Er, Meg? This one’s all yours.” It was the Musician. He wouldn’t elaborate, so I went upstairs to the bathroom. There, soaking in water up to his neck

was my smiling toddler. Floating all around him were mini poop logs. Welcome to my potty training nightmare. They forgot to ask him if he needed to go to the bathroom before sinking him in soothing, bowel releasing water.

It was too much for the bachelors and they fled. By the time I cleaned everything up, got Esah back into a fresh tub, and finally to bed; it had taken two hours more than if I had done it in the first place. Note to self, keep bachelors away from the kid.

That Friday, it was obvious they wanted to do something for me to make up for, well, everything. They were going out partying, but before they left The Musician lent me his truck and video card to go to the store and rent a movie. Esah had fallen asleep early, no doubt exhausted from coming up with ways to make me lose my mind.

I had completely lost touch with the film business. I didn’t know anything about the new movies that were out. Now, I was in single working mom wonderland. As I searched the shelves at the beach video store, one title caught my eye, *The Joy Luck Club*. Wow, sounded perfect. I wanted Joy, I needed Luck. It was about women and their kids, perfect! I raced home and put the movie in.

For the next two hours I watched Chinese mothers in the most impossible situations imaginable: mothers abandoning babies, mothers forced to kill their own children, moms facing the worst nightmares possible.

I sobbed so hard I almost choked up a lung. The surfers came home and stared at me in bewilderment.

"This is your idea of fun?"

But it worked. Seeing women in far more dire circumstances snapped me out of my self pity. If those women could face their hardship with dignity and honor, I better do the same.

I had read a couple of quotes by Paramahansa Yogananda, founder of the Self Realization Fellowship (SRF) while browsing in their bookstore in the neighboring town of Encinitas. One quote stood out in my mind.

"We have more ability to overcome obstacles than we have obstacles to overcome."

As hard as that was to believe, I was starting to realize it was true. People all over the world were facing challenges. But somehow, many were making it through even the toughest tests. Meditation had always helped me, and I realized I needed to kick it up a notch. I had been circling around the SRF for years and realized I wanted to see what they were really all about.

Esah and I walked over one afternoon and Esah stopped abruptly in front of their bookstore window. Pictures of Enlightened Masters gazed mystically at us.

"I know that guy," said the munchkin holding my hand.

I looked closer at the gentle face and flowing white mane of the Swami known as Sri Yukteswar, Yogananda's teacher.

"You know him?"

Esah nodded emphatically. This was new. I had no idea where this was coming from, maybe a past life.

“Would you like his picture?”

More nodding. We went inside and I paid for the photo. For myself I bought *The Autobiography of a Yogi* by Paramahansa Yogananda. It is a beautiful story of one man’s search for the meaning of life. It led him to Enlightenment, in effect, winning this video game of life. He came to America in an effort to blend the materialism of the West with the spirituality of the East. He taught an ancient meditation practice called Kriya Yoga, aimed at helping everyone get closer to their own personal truth.

“*Even a little practice of this technique will save you from great fear in this lifetime,*” he had promised, way back in the 30s.

Lord knows I was sick of being terrified every day. I decided I wanted to learn. The icing on the cake was that he had received his name from the immortal, Mahavatar Babaji.

I began attending Sunday meditations, and Esah learned to meditate with other 3 year olds in the Sunday School. It was mind blowing to see a room full of toddlers peacefully meditating. While he floated in toddler bliss, I was in my own version of heaven sitting amongst an eclectic group of meditators comprised of Buddhist Monks from Japan, Jews, Catholics, Agnostics, and hippies in the main temple.

I signed up for the Kriya Yoga lessons, which were mailed to me every two weeks, and began my quest for the meaning of life. The lessons stressed the importance of meditating every morning and every evening. I was already getting up at 5:30 a.m., so it meant I had to start getting up a half hour earlier. It was grueling at first, but gradually I found myself craving it. My morning meditation was my way of telling the world we were going to do it my way. It limited the number of idiots who could mess with me. I liked it.

When we were homeless, I felt my soul had been ripped out of my body and given a good shaking. And the shaking never stopped. I used to wake up with a feeling of dread, carried it with me all day, and fell asleep with it.

As the months passed and my meditations became deeper, the shaking stopped. The chattering in my head died down and with relief I found my thoughts were few and far between. Instead of a head full of news bulletins, gossip, and other people's ideas, I regained control. When I wanted quiet, I got quiet.

The teachings had originated with Babaji, whose instructions to mankind were simple and timeless: practice truth, simplicity, and love. Well, I was living simply enough, our net income was $800 a month. I was struggling hard to find the truth about life. Now, I just had to get rid of the hate, and fear, and learn to love again.

Disciples of Yogananda who lived at the SRF ashram were called ashramites and were available for free counseling sessions. I desperately needed someone to talk to. I was still under the constant threat of running into the version of John that was unhinged and murderous.

So one day, I took time away from making topiaries, borrowed the greenhouse truck, and drove down the hill to the SRF. Inside the pristine white walls of the ashram were the most amazing tropical gardens imaginable. The men and women living there tended the gardens as part of their daily meditation.

Stepping out of the hot California sun, I entered a world that could have been straight from *Jungle Book*. Tall palm trees shaded the walk way that was lined with Birds of Paradise, massive ferns, flowers of every color and shape, weaving around ponds of giant koi fish.

I made my way to the main office, and they escorted me into a quiet book lined library to wait. As I sat on the comfortable old couch, looking at the statues of Buddha, Shiva, and saints from every religion in the world, I felt the immense comfort offered by these beings. I never wanted to leave. Here, I was safe. I looked out the window at the happy residents, on their way to meditate, do chores, all in the safety of this ashram.

What I wouldn't have given to trade places with them. They didn't have to worry about paying rent, buying groceries, dodging every scam artist in town. But the universe, probably sensing my desire to hide when times got hard, had played its trump card and given me a child. I guess I would have to continue slugging it out in the real world.

A strong vibrant woman strode into the room to talk to me. She must have read my mind, because she got right down to business. "Too many people want to sweep the floors and pray to God, but that's not reality. You have a son to support and put through college. Are you making enough money to do that?"

I shook my head stupidly.

"Then you need to get a better job."

I told her about my fear of John, and she told me an astounding thing. She said I wasn't allowing him to change, because he was trapped in my image of him. She said it was important to remember who he had been, and only focus on that. It would allow his soul to become whole again.

"Wouldn't it be wonderful, for your son, if you could

invite his father over for a cup of tea?"

I thought she had rocks in her head. I was dealing with a crazy man, and she was talking about tea parties.

But when I left I couldn't forget what she said. I started saying affirmations out loud, about forgiving John, but my heart wasn't in it.

"I release all that is unlike love," I babbled as I cleaned house, worked in the greenhouses, and ran errands on our bike. One day while I was in the greenhouses finishing off a giant Fu Lion, one of the Mexican women came up to me and told me about the Montessori Preschool that was located in the greenhouse district. It was for migrant worker's kids. I was Canadian, and therefore, a migrant worker.

I decided to investigate. One lunch hour I walked over to a cozy nest of one room cottages surrounded by beautiful gardens and playgrounds. All of the greenhouse workers tended the gardens here and donated plants being throwing out at the greenhouses. Under the gentle nurturing of the parents and children, all homeless plants quickly flourished and became show pieces.

The Migrant Montessori Preschool was established to make sure migrant worker's kids entered school on par with their American counterparts who had, in most cases, been in daycares and preschools getting socialized. I had actually checked into the cost of such a preschool before the "troubles", but the tuition was more than my rent, so out of the question.

I love the Montessori method of teaching, which allows each child to progress at their own pace. Now here was a chance my son could attend one for free.

With fingers and toes crossed, I went in to meet the head mistress. She was Mexican, fluently bilingual and ran the three cottage operation with amazing efficiency. She spoke to me in perfect English, without a trace of an accent, switching to flawless Spanish whenever one of the preschool teachers came in with a question.

I filled out some forms and sat nervously waiting for her decision. She looked at me and shook her head.

"You have a greater need than most of our families here. Usually grandparents or siblings are around who can watch the kids during the day. You have nobody. How have you been managing to work?"

"I bring him with me."

She smiled and put out her hand. "We've never had a Canadian before. Welcome to Montessori."

I shook her hand, then grabbed her and hugged her. A giant cloud lifted. Here was a safe, creative Mecca of learning for Esah. Here he could play with kids his own age while I worked, and become bilingual to boot. I began to realize that surrendering to Existence was the best move I ever made.

18

FORGIVENESS

The next couple of years passed quietly and simply. As soon as I developed a daily meditation routine, the mishaps and accidents of the past stopped, synchronicity reigned. Little by little, I learned how to live in society again. I attended parent meetings at night at the preschool, hunkered down in the tiny classroom chair like some sort of praying Mantis, surrounded by diminutive Mexican women. Esah became fluently bilingual and blossomed at the peaceful school.

We finally stopped rooming with other people and found a place of our own. It was a beautiful little studio cabin located on the grounds of an old monastery. First it had been a Catholic Mission, then a Buddhist monastery. And it was across the tracks from the SRF temple.

High white walls surrounded the property with all our little cabins nestled against the inner wall. In the centre were ancient fruit trees, rose bushes, and a fish pond full of deep orange gold fish. Our cabin was sunk into a hill by the back wall. As a result I could walk onto the roof from the back and see the ocean from this vantage point. And right in front of our cottage were three old, overgrown topiaries.

Inside the cabin was one big room, actually bigger than the garden shed Esah was born in. The kitchen was along one wall, a walk in closet at the back. The only separate room was the tiny bathroom with a shower stall.

Our next door neighbor was the lucky one in the garden shed. He was a young paramedic, and quite popular with the ladies. I often got the giggles when I saw him bring home a date. His space was so narrow two people couldn't stand next to each other inside. I guess it made jumping into bed even more appealing.

The other renters were Mexican families also working in the greenhouses and flower fields. We would open our doors on the weekends and release a tidal wave of kids into the central yard to play. There was a beautiful energy around the place. It had been settled as a Catholic Mission in the 1920s, but they chose a woman to lead them. Rome refused to ordain a female priest, they refused to give her up, Rome excommunicated the whole lot of them, and they became the first free mission in the United States. After a few decades it became Buddhist, and finally, our home.

My spiritual path took a giant leap forward when I was finally invited to be initiated into the Kriya Yoga tradition that I had been practicing through the SRF. The ceremony was scheduled to take place at the temple Paramahamsa Yogananda first established when he arrived in California. It was a beautiful white jewel located smack in the middle of the Hollywood Strip, north of us in Los Angeles. When he established it Hollywood was a beautiful, small town. Now the temple was surrounded by strip joints and tattoo parlors.

I read a story about Yogananda standing outside of the Hollywood temple one summer day, the only dark skinned person for miles around, when a white haired Bible thumping woman stormed up to him and screamed, "You're going to burn in hell!"

He smiled and replied, "Where do you think we are?"

The night of our initiation, my friends and I drove the three hours up to Los Angeles from Encinitas. We entered the temple with our offerings of fruit and flowers. What followed was one of the most mystical evenings I had ever experienced. Ancient Sanskrit chants made my entire body vibrate. Smiling, glowing people threw rose petals on me, and finally we went up to the Senior Swamis one at a time for energy darshan. If only my wedding ceremonies had carried this much reverence, this much meaning, maybe the marriages would have had a chance. I felt myself lifted above the mundane drama of the Earth and float gently in some space beyond. And I couldn't stop laughing! It all seemed like such a joke, this melodrama we create and live in!

When we left at the end of the evening, I felt I had a spiritual army watching my back now. Whatever life wanted to throw at me, bring it on! We hopped in the car and headed south back to Encinitas. Just as we came abreast of Disneyland, a barrage of fireworks went off. We laughed hysterically as the whole universe celebrated our initiation with us.

*****

Now that Esah and I were no longer nomadic and had a place to call our own, it was time for a new kitten to show up. Esah kept talking about how we were going to find a Rainbow Kitty, and he loved to chatter away about it as I drove him to preschool in the topiary van. One morning just after I dropped him off, I heard a kitten crying behind one of the school buildings.

In my best "come hither" voice I called "Here Kitty, Kitty, Kitty!"

A small multi-colored kitten flew around the corner and down the hill to where I was parked. She looked about six months old and she was in rough shape.

Judging from the matted coat and fleas, she had been alone for a long time.

"Are you Esah's Rainbow Kitty?"

She stared at me with gorgeous green eyes, rubbed my leg affectionately, and jumped into the van. She was like an old friend who had been waiting for me to show up. She rode shotgun in Esah's car seat while we sailed back down the hill to our cabin. I had once again been taking care of strays and finding them homes, so I had a litter and food in our storage shed.

I was late for work so I hustled her inside, set up her stuff and gave her the discount tour. "There's your food, your litter, we sleep here, see you at five."

When Esah and I got home that evening she was contentedly curled up on the futon, purring.

Esah lifted her up in a gigantic hug. "Rainbow Kitty!"

His soul mate had come home.

As I got to know my neighbors, I was struck by what a loving, graceful community the Mexicans had. They watched out for each other, found regular reasons to celebrate life, and loved their kids. When Christmas rolled around, they really kicked into high gear. Decorations were put up and plans were made for a band to come and play.

Esah and I had a simpler day planned. When we got up, Esah had three presents nestled under our small ivy topiary tree. He opened them carefully; thrilled with each modest one. With no ceremony left other than to say a prayer of thanks for being off the street, safe and warm, we went to the beach to play.

Returning home that afternoon, the place was buzzing. The women had noticed that Esah and I were alone and they all agreed something had to be done. Two huge plates piled high with Christmas dinners arrived at our front door. Dumbstruck, we joined them on their patios and stuffed ourselves. While Esah played with the kids I practiced my limited Spanish with the other mothers. They were astounded that I was alone, and it was obvious they couldn't understand the American culture that would leave oddballs like us stranded.

Then the band arrived. Mariachi music filled the night along with the laughter of the families in our sanctuary. After I got Esah snuggled into bed with Rainbow Kitty, I went outside and up onto my roof. I sat facing the ocean, watching the moon reflected off the peaceful water, and sent up a silent prayer of thanks for one of the best Christmases I had ever had. And I felt Existence thank me back for playing the game so well.

*****

As the New Year unfolded, Esah started acting out. He had witnessed intense scenes of violence and screaming between his father and me. All that energy had been taken in by his small body, but it had nowhere to go. So he started biting me. Everyone who is on the receiving end of anger has to release it somehow, this was his way.

There was one renter on our property whose space was an office. He was a Jungian Analyst, trained at the C.G. Jung Institute of Zurich. The Jungian loved taking breaks from his clients and wandering out to the fish pond to philosophize with Esah about fish, bugs, and life. Esah would babble happily to him unaware he was being analyzed to within an inch of his Dog Boy of Leucadia life.

One day I spoke to The Jungian about his practice. He explained that he used "Sand Play Therapy" to help his clients uncover deeply hidden issues. He showed me his office. It was lined with shelves holding every type of action figure imaginable. Cowboys rode on one shelf, monsters on another, anything you could dream of had an action figure to represent it. Two square sandboxes on wheels sat in the middle of the room. The Jungian explained that it was just as significant *what* people chose to play with, as *how* they played.

With my heart in my throat, I asked him if he ever helped children. He nodded and explained children were the easiest to work with because they hadn't built walls and moats around their issues; they said whatever came to mind. I asked him if he could help Esah, and held my breath.

"Yes," he replied, "What can you afford?"

"I know you make over $100 an hour and I don't want to insult you."

"That's not what I asked you," he said carefully, "I asked what you could afford."

"Twenty dollars a week?" Even as I said it, I was trying to think how we could do with less groceries to even pay twenty dollars. But this was one of those moments when I knew a massive gift was being given to us. My son was being offered a way out of his anger. I had to make it work.

He smiled at me. "I would be willing to see Esah every Thursday for a half hour for twenty dollars."

We shook hands and watched my curly haired munchkin careening down the hill on his Tonka truck, runners dragging on the sidewalk in an attempt to stop himself before he went headfirst down the steep stairs at the end of the path. He screeched to a halt just in time. His buddies cheered. The Jungian smiled.

"See you Thursday."

When the appointed day rolled around, I explained to Esah that he was going to play in that amazing office across the garden. Esah excitedly went inside. I waved at the Jungian and left. That night the Jungian called to tell me how it went.

Esah picked out two, two-headed dragons and a small baby dragon. He buried the baby dragon in the sand, while the two big ones roared at each other and battled. Well, I didn't need to be Jung to figure that one out. Esah viewed both his dad and me as fighting monsters, while he hid in the sand. I felt awful.

Esah never saw money change hands. The Jungian called me after Esah was asleep to report on the sessions. But I didn't need the official perspective. When Esah came home after his first session he gave me a huge hug and said, "I love you, Mom."

Subconsciously I believe he knew he was being helped. He was being shown a way out of the turmoil going on inside him. The Jungian explained that being a safe adult meant Esah could roar and holler at him without fear of being hurt. He was safe with this therapist, free to act out all the anger, frustration, and helplessness he had felt through the first years of his life, and let it go.

After a few months Esah finally began playing with normal human figures, doing happy things, and the therapy was over. I will be eternally grateful to The Jungian for the gift he gave my child and me. I believe that's why Esah was such a loving teenager, he had nothing left to act out.

One day the therapist's curiosity got to him and he asked about John's art. "Is it drug art? Or real art?"

I showed him photos from one of John's shows, including a self-portrait he did of himself holding Esah as a baby. The Jungian shook his head sadly. "He's got a real gift. Unfortunately the line between being gifted and insane is a very fine one."

I continued working on my own state of mind, saying affirmations out loud, hoping to heal. Then one day, an amazing thing happened. I realized that after years of robotically chanting that I had forgiven John, I finally meant it.

I missed the John I fell in love with on Venice Beach; the amazing man who helped everyone, who made me laugh, who let me be who I wanted to be without judgment. And as soon as I changed my mind about him, he reappeared. And he was that man again. The madness had left him, and all I felt was love.

Confucius once said, *"To be wronged is nothing unless you continue to remember it."*

I had held on to my anger for John far too long. Never again would I be so reluctant to forgive. One day I came around a corner and there he was, walking a friend's dog. We surprised each other, then smiled. All the anger was gone, we were genuinely happy to see each other. For awhile, at least, we could be friends again.

That simple act of forgiveness set an entire string of events into motion that would change the course of our lives. I realized working in the greenhouses had no future for me. I was being paid by the topiary, but that included lifting huge bales of moss, lugging massive rebar frames, and basically doing any heavy lifting the store owner couldn't do. With a heavy heart, I turned in my resignation and prayed that God would let me be a writer.

I helped the shop get through the busy Christmas rush, and by New Year's Eve, I was unemployed. The SRF temple had a wonderful tradition. They held a New Year's meditation which began at 11:30 pm New Year's Eve, and continued through into New Year's Day, and my birthday. Years of celebrating my birthday with drunks had taught me to avoid parties at all costs. I decided a meditation was the jump start my new writing career needed.

I walked through the dark streets of Encinitas that New Year's Eve night with Esah snuggled against my shoulder. He had already been asleep for hours as I made the ten block pilgrimage. I was pooped by the time I reached the front door.

An usher looked at me in dismay. "No children are allowed!"

"But he's sleeping!"

"I'm sorry, that's the rule. He might wake up and disturb everyone."

I sat down on the front steps with a thud, trying in vain not to cry. People walked past me, murmuring amongst themselves. I had a flash of being homeless again. Of being stranded while people with lives hurried by, whispering about me. But I was wrong. Everyone was talking about me, but in a good way. They were trying to find a way for me to stay. The usher re-emerged breathlessly from inside with a key in his hand.

"Quick, follow me!"

We raced next door into a little vestibule. He unlocked a door and I entered a small room with a scattering of chairs and tons of toys, the "Kid Room". It was only used during Sunday services. He turned on the television and I saw the live feed from inside the temple. I thanked him gratefully and he left.

I put Esah on the ground in front of me, wrapped in my coat. I listened to the music float out of the television, and smiled. I wouldn't have to celebrate New Year's alone after all.

"*Enthusiastically expect the best!*" was one of my favorite sayings by Paramahamsa Yogananda.

And that's what I did. I meditated away my life as a laborer. I meditated away the homelessness. I meditated away my fear. That soft feeling, like a caress, enveloped me. The more I learned to still myself, the greater the peace.

At midnight I heard the locals banging pans, and a few guns being fired into the air. Such a lovely tradition, dodging bullets as they plummet back to Earth, "Happy New Year!"

When the service was over, I took out our last dollar and put it in the small offering dish. I remembered the Voice telling me not to be a beggar in life, to demand my rights as a child of God. I yelled my New Year's Resolution to the Universe. "I want to be paid as a writer!"

I picked Esah up and walked home. He didn't seem to weigh anything at all.

19

THE SERBIAN

The first week in January a friend of mine called and asked if I would consider cleaning her father's house. "I know you want to write, but I can't find anyone to come and clean. It's cash. Just something to help you get by until a writing job shows up."

Her father, The Serbian, was a famous artist who had been named one of California's Living Treasures. He was a painter, sculptor, jeweler, and all round Renaissance Man. Hmm, writer, cleaning lady, writer. Oh well, I decided it wouldn't hurt to keep myself busy and make some cash. Plus her dad was an interesting guy. Who knew, it might be a fun day.

When I quit the greenhouse, Esah no longer qualified for the Montessori preschool. The teachers wished us a tearful farewell, and assured me Esah had completed all of the learning stations. He was ready for kindergarten in the fall. It meant we were travelling as a team again, and I was grateful for his company. I had missed being around his joyful energy.

We were picked up the next day for the cleaning gig and driven up the hill to The Serb's property. It was an old avocado ranch when he bought it. That was one of the things I loved about Encinitas. It was full of poinsettia ranches, begonia gardens, and flower fields; farmers.

The Serbian had bought his property in the fifties and pretty much left it in its natural state. His white stucco bungalow with the red Spanish tile roof was perched above a canyon alive with overgrown Jade plants, cactus plants and towering Eucalyptus trees. His daughter lived next door in his old art studio cabin with her son, Esah's best friend. It was down the path from the main house.

The bungalow still had a modest exterior. Once inside, however, you walked into a work of art. Massive hand carved wooden doors guarded the entry ways, huge oil paintings adorned every wall; sculptures and model boats hid under piles of papers. Even the kitchen floor was a handmade marble tile mosaic of sea life. He had created his own Museum of Art.

After a quick introduction, The Serb grunted at me and went out onto the patio to read. The house was in an "L" shape that bordered a beautiful stone patio and hot tub. An outdoor shower nestled in amongst the trailing vines and shrubs.

The Serb walked with a cane, and I could tell from the piles of dusty drawings, newspapers, and books that he had lived alone for some time. His days of being an artist were long gone. The Serb's skin was permanently burnished from years of living outside swimming, skiing, and searching for inspiration in Nature. His shock of white hair and electric brown eyes made him a handsome man, even as a senior.

I found it soothing to clean the one level home. It was far enough from the Pacific Coast Highway that I couldn't hear the traffic. The only sound was the wind moving the giant Eucalyptus trees that surrounded the bungalow. Faintly I could hear Esah and his buddy yelling and laughing down in the canyon.

Once I was done, The Serb paid me cash and his daughter drove us home. It was a wonderful day, despite the fact that I wasn't writing. Cash in your pocket is always a good thing. The next week I was called again to clean. No writing gig had materialized, so Esah and I went up the hill to his canyon home again.

As his daughter drove us she looked at me in amazement. "I was surprised he wanted you back."

"Really? Why?"

"He usually eats people alive."

"Great. Why didn't you tell me that before?"

"I was afraid you wouldn't come."

This time The Serb hovered around a little more, finally settling at the kitchen table where Esah was drawing. "Vat can you tell me 'bout dis?" The Serb demanded with his strong Serbian accent. He glared at Esah.

My son, quite frankly, had seen scarier. He patiently explained his art to the old fart. "It's a palm tree, and this is my cat." With those simple words, a new friendship began.

The next time I cleaned his place, The Serb started talking to me, and I actually made him laugh a few times. He said he heard I was a writer and asked to read a sample of my work. I decided the Gold Rush piece about my grandparent's life in the Klondike Gold Rush would be the most interesting for a man with his background.

The Serb had suffered immense hardships in concentration camps during World War II. I thought he might find my grandparents' story interesting, since it also dealt with surviving against the odds. I was right, he loved it. And then my world changed again, he asked me to write his memoirs.

People think that surrendering to Existence means losing control of your life. This was the exact opposite to what I was experiencing. Every since I had surrendered to Existence that stormy night in the abandoned motel room, synchronicity and auspiciousness had become a way of life - from my son being able to attend the Montessori school, to finally being paid to write full time.

I held my breath as the Serb explained that some of his jewelry was in the Smithsonian and they had been hounding him to get his story written down. Problem was he didn't know any writers, until me. I realized The Serbian was such a recluse, it was impossible for him to meet writers. By getting to know me first, an element of trust had been built. The universe was once again moving the chess pieces around the board to help me out.

I felt a little nudge and wink from Yogananda. "*Enthusiastically expect the best*".

The Serbian asked me what I would charge to interview him and write the book. I was tempted to say five dollars an hour I was so desperate to do the project. Instead, I took a breath and I told him I'd have to think about it. I meditated that night and the friendly Voice in my head came back. It reminded me that if anyone knew the value of art, it was The Serbian. He had been paid a fortune for his creations; he would expect me to value myself enough to set a reasonable price.

The next time I saw him, I stated my price, four times what I had been making in the greenhouses. I felt like I'd asked for the moon. He didn't blink. We had a deal. Our days became quiet, contemplative times of storytelling. I took him to places he loved, since he was easier to interview when he was happy. The Serb, Esah, and I became a strange, yet comforting little faux family unit.

One afternoon Esah and I decided to treat ourselves and go down the coast to Del Mar on the bus. We wandered the streets of the quaint town, visited the beach, then bought ourselves some fresh fruit and sweets from a local produce market. When we got on the bus to go back up the coastline, we ended up sitting next to a young woman and her mixed race daughter.

The little girl was outgoing and curious, asking us what we had in the bag. Her mother stared out the window, and I could see the foundations of her being were crumbling. Esah saw it as well, and we answered the call from Existence to help. Esah took a basket of strawberries and crackers out of our bag, and had a picnic with the little girl. Her mother tried hard to hide her shame that her daughter was so hungry.

I gently began speaking to her and found out I was looking at a replay of the same thing that had happened to me years before. She was on her way to the welfare office to apply for aid. I remembered the day I finally admitted I needed help, and Esah and I had spent a gut wrenching day in the hell hole that was the local welfare office. It took all day to get in line, get a number, and wait in the waiting room for an interview. I remembered going to the bathroom so I could sit alone in a stall and cry. It was the most humbling, humiliating day of my life. And now I was looking at a young girl, from Australia, going through the same torture.

I told her to be strong, that this was a test, and we are never given more than we can handle. I told her I had been there and survived it. This shocked her. Looking at me she saw a middle class woman with money and a happy kid. I had successfully hidden the homeless label that used to brand me.

When it was time for us to get off the bus Esah nudged me and gently opened my wallet. In it was a five dollar bill and a twenty. His fingers lightly touched the twenty and I nodded. He took it out and handed it to the little girl. Her mother broke down in tears.

I felt a soft sigh from the Universe. I had been able to pay forward the twenty I had been given by that man in the Laundromat so many years ago.

*****

As the spring turned to summer The Serb's health deteriorated rapidly. Starving for years during the war, stumbling through the countryside of Yugoslavia with the Partisan Army, had seriously broken down his body. He told me the Red Cross had dropped food supplies to his unit, but they didn't use parachutes on the plummeting provisions back then. As a result, there were scores of deaths from falling pasta.

"I guess, in a vay, dey ver putting us out of our misery."

He would drive down the hill to pick us up, and quite frankly, his driving scared the crap out of me. He was always going up over the curb, straddling two lanes on the freeway, and misjudging his distances. I asked his daughter why she let him drive. She whimpered that she wouldn't dare tell him what to do. This man who was larger than life intimidated her. To me, he was just an old, frail man. The next time he picked us up I confronted him.

"You know what? Why don't you let me drive from now on. You can call me anytime you want and I'll drive you, deal?"

A look of relief filled his face as he handed over the keys. "I scare de crap out of myself drivin' dis ting."

Who knew? We were on the same page. At first his daughter was in shock, but then, she realized there was an opportunity at hand. One night she invited Esah and me for dinner. It was a wonderful night. We ate in the old art studio overlooking the ravine. Eucalyptus filled the air. We watched our sons play together. Suddenly she became serious.

"Would you be interested in moving in with dad?"

I was completely caught off guard. It was one thing to spend four hours a day with him, then retreat to the sanctuary of my own home; quite another to be with him around the clock.

"He's starting to have small strokes. Something could happen to him alone up there. We need someone to move in with him."

"Why don't you?" I was more than slightly confused.

"Oh, I will. We're going to renovate the house so there's room for all of us. Then you and Esah could move into the art studio."

I didn't quite understand how she and her son took up more space than Esah and me, but I let my mind ponder the idea. The art studio was my idea of heaven. It was a separate adobe style building on stilts overlooking the ravine, a huge deck snuggled against the entire perimeter. The massive studio cabin had a fireplace separating the workshop from the living quarters. It bigger than anything Esah and I had lived in yet.

But first, I had to move in with the Serb. There could be all kinds of tension around this. I was about to decline when she pulled out her trump card. “Oh, we found these rolled up in his art supplies. I thought you’d like to have them.”

She held out two beautiful black and white photographs; one of my guru, Paramahansa Yogananda, the other of his teacher, Sri Yukteswar. The latter was the man Esah recognized when he was a toddler. I was speechless. This whole clan was atheist. What the hell were they doing with pictures of my gurus? I felt the universe laughing at me as Yogananda smiled from the old photograph.

“Alright, we’ll do it.”

*****

It was sad packing up our place in the old monastery. It had been our sanctuary for years, and Esah had made a lot of friends there. But his best friend was the Serb’s grandson and he would be living right next door. He couldn’t wait to move.

Our rooms were the two back bedrooms in the old house where the Serb’s daughters had grown up. The simple white walls and hardwood floors were accented by the stunning views of the property. It immediately felt like home. Rainbow Kitty tentatively entered the premises. She didn’t need to worry, The Serb was thrilled to have a pet around. Having voices, bodies, and even fur back in his house filled him with peace. It was the first time I had seen him really happy.

Our first morning in our new home I hunted around the kitchen getting dishes, cereal and milk out for Esah. I set him up at the kitchen table. I thought I would let the Serb sleep in. As I bent over the cat’s dish, I heard Esah’s frantic whisper.

“Old Man Winkie!!!”

I looked up in time to see The Serb, buck naked, rumble by the table. His "bits and pieces" swung dangerously close to Esah's cereal bowl. I gasped, The Serb glared, Esah put both his hands over the bowl to protect it from being tea bagged by the old guy. We stared at each other in horror until The Serb had passed. As soon as he was out of earshot I grabbed the phone and called his daughter.

"Your dad's running around the house naked!"

"So?"

"So, Esah's freaking out!"

"He's a nudist. He always walked around like that when we were kids. Esah will get used to it."

Funny, that wasn't in the brochure. I hung up in exasperation. This would take more adjusting than I thought. The Serb had survived on instincts his whole life, and quickly picked up on the fact that we weren't interested in seeing his "meat and two vegs" at breakfast. He condescended to putting on some shorts when we were around.

Eventually, we all got used to being together, and it was time for Esah to start school. We were just a few blocks from the elementary school The Serb's girls had attended, and now Esah would be going to kindergarten there with his best friend.

I walked him up the hill that first day and met his teacher, a sweet young thing who was also experiencing her first day of school. She was a last minute addition to the curriculum; her class was in a portable structure behind the main school. She had lovingly made curtains for the classroom; her husband put up the shelves. Esah couldn't have been in better hands.

But that was all lost on me. As I waved goodbye to him and stood in the parking lot, I broke down. The tension and struggle of his first five years rushed me. I don't think I believed we would make it this far. A few other moms were also bidding tearful goodbyes, and one gal, a potter, caught my eye. Kindred creative souls, we went for coffee, and a new phase of my life began.

With Esah busy all day, and a writing job at home, I began to relax and let the stress out of my system. Long walks with new friends, reading books, renting movies with the Serb, made me feel like my old self again. For years back in Canada I had all of these things, and took them for granted. Having money in my pocket, a job to complain about, girlfriends to laugh with, were things I expected as my right as a human being. When it was all taken away I realized what gifts the Universe had been throwing at me, and never once had I said "Thank you".

The time with The Serbian brought a sense of belonging, gratitude, and family that I hadn't had since my first years with John. The days developed a gentle rhythm. We prowled his favorite haunts. Most mornings began at an outdoor café with a chocolate croissant and orange juice. We would sit in the sun while he slipped into the past and remembered his life. Looking back after decades of success, he was able to laugh at some of the more bizarre memories.

One of his escapes from a concentration camp was the result of his keen observation, and ingenuity. He said everyone knew you could buy a Frenchman with a pack of cigarettes. One camp he was imprisoned in was being supplied by the French. The Serb bartered and traded until he got a carton of cigarettes through the camp's black market. He used it to bribe a French driver and drove out of the camp sitting in the front passenger seat. The sheer audacity of the move was so unexpected, the guards never thought to check him.

Living with the old warrior, seeing what he had accomplished as a refugee from a war-torn country, made me realize I was being too timid when it came to my own dreams.

As we talked about it, this survivor of concentration camps, starvation, and his wife's death, looked at me and asked a simple question. "Vy not make your own movie? Vat's de vorst that could happen?"

He was right. I was so paralyzed with unknown fears; believing it was impossible for a writer to learn to make a film, I hadn't even tried. Put simply like that, what was the worst that could go wrong? I certainly wouldn't end up homeless, bleeding in the gutter. It was just art. I didn't know how to start this adventure, so I waited for a sign.

One morning I sat next to Esah's bed while he floated out of his dream world. He opened his eyes and spoke to me in a faraway voice. "Mom, you don't have to worry about me anymore. I have a golden angel that lives in my heart and tells me everything I need to know."

Heavy words from a five year old. "Well, that's wonderful, Sweetie. Do I have an angel too?"

"Yup, he's really big. His name is Goliath and he's standing right behind you."

Something crawled up my spine while my hair stood at attention. I turned slowly to look. Nothing. But I knew he was right. I remembered when Esah was a baby he was always laughing and smiling at something over my shoulder and above me. He wasn't looking at me. I guess it was Goliath. I figured, with a guy like that on my side, what did I have to lose? Time for me and Goliath to make a film. But where to start?

One day The Serb and I were prowling around a local bookstore when one title caught my eye, *Rebel Without A Crew* by filmmaker Robert Rodriquez. He was an indie film phenomenon who had made his first film on a few thousand dollars, then written a book to explain how to do it. I grabbed it greedily. This was my ticket. I bought the book, rushed us out of the store, and practically threw the Serb into the passenger seat of his old Saab. I couldn't wait to get home and start reading. The Serb joked that it must be quite the treasure. I assured him, it was.

Inspired by the sheer audacity of Rodriquez and his quest to make a film, I followed his instructions to the letter. First, I printed up cheap business cards announcing to the world I was a filmmaker. Next, it was time to phone people I knew and try to convince them to invest in my project. I felt the best strategy was to ask for an amount I knew people could afford without putting any stress on their finances.

I got up early every morning and meditated, asking for the names of people to call. Within moments of making the call, each person agreed to invest.

One friend brought me to tears when she said, "I've always believed in you. I always knew you could do it." To realize so many people back in Canada were supporting me was overwhelming.

Next I needed a bank account to convert all these out of country checks into cash. When John vanished, he took all our money out of the bank the same day my payments hit for rent, utilities, and bills. The bank tried to help by covering my bills. But when I became homeless I couldn't repay them. I had a debt of several thousand dollars.

I phoned the bank and wrote down the exact amount I owed. They quoted a reference number to me and I began saving. When my income tax refund arrived I had enough. Esah and I headed out to the bank one bright sunny morning. We entered the building and all my confidence fled. I became paralyzed by a panic attack. Gone were the days of walking in wearing a business suit, having funds at my fingertips. I felt everyone in there knew I was a homie and didn't belong. I slunk over to the customer service rep, and whispered my situation to her.

She smiled kindly. "Well, let's look it up."

She checked my reference number, our names, social security numbers, everything. It was nowhere to be found. She suggested we go ahead and open an account; the computer would be sure to red flag me as a credit risk. I nodded, heart pounding as she input all the information.

A huge "WELCOME" message appeared on the screen.

"Guess that money is the seed money for your film!"

Thunderstruck, I went through the motions of opening an account, and depositing the money I had brought to pay the debt. As a final hug from the Universe, the bank offered to wave the waiting period on foreign checks, so that I would have access to my investors' funds immediately. I think the tellers were even more excited than I was that an adventure was afoot! Thanking her profusely I took Esah by the hand and staggered out of the bank. There was a roaring in my ears and I had to sit down on the curb. Esah hugged me.

"What's wrong, Mommy?"

"You don't understand what just happened in there. God just erased our debt."

In my mind's eye, a giant hand holding a long yellow 2H pencil came out of the sky and pointed the eraser at the bank.

"She's been really good," it said as it erased my entry in the ledger. It had paid me for helping a lonely old man.

*****

The thirty minute script I wrote for the film was a day in the life of John's camp of homies on Venice Beach. I had written the feature length version when John and I first got together. I remember John reading this account of his life, and shaking his head at my dialogue.

"Now I know that's what your white, middle class brain thought you heard, but what they really said was..." And he would correct it for me.

I had tried to get Hollywood interested but everyone declined. "Great writing, but no one will touch this; too many taboos." Apparently the homeless, a white woman with a black man, and the plight of Vietnam Vets, was not anything Hollywood wanted to produce. I was on my own.

Now that I was attempting to film it, I was eager to have John involved. The Serbian wanted to meet the artist who was Esah's dad and encouraged me to have him come by and visit. At first I was worried about what would happen when their two worlds collided. I shouldn't have. One artist meeting another creates a universe all of its own.

John had been living with a friend down the hill, so I tracked him down and invited him over. I sat on the front step and waited. I watched his lean frame and mane of dreadlocks come up the hill. He still had that easy, homie walk that had carried him for miles and miles over a lifetime. His bags of many colors bumped against his youthful looking body. From a distance, like many homies, he resembled a teenager. It was only when he got close that the fine lines and signs of grey in his hair could be seen.

I introduced him to the Serb. They wandered through the house while The Serb talked about the huge oil paintings on the walls. John practically melted as he admired the paintings, the Serb's handmade model boats, the sculptures. After hours discussing art they moved to the back patio and I served them lunch. John had brought a huge, African Djembe drum with him. He showed it to The Serb, carefully explaining how the skin was put on, how it needs to be heated before playing. I watched them, hunched over the drum, kindred spirits.

After the visit was over, we watched John disappear down the hill, The Serbian shook his head sadly and said it was hard to explain what war did to a man, especially artists like him and John. Then he said something startling, "If I hadn't married a wealthy woman, I would have wound up like him."

*****

The day finally arrived when The Serbian's memoirs were finished. I had gone over the manuscript several times, double checking facts, finding photos and artwork to illustrate each section.

One night when Esah was asleep I wheeled The Serbian to the kitchen table and placed the final manuscript in front of him. He had just returned from the hospital after yet another stroke and was now permanently wheelchair bound. One side was paralyzed, leaving his shaky left hand to turn the pages of his life story.

He asked to be left alone with it. I went out the kitchen door to the patio and sat under the starlit sky, listening for any sound that might let me know if he approved of what I'd written. He sat there for hours, turning page after page, the sound of his weeping echoing out the window and into the night. The release for him was huge. To see it written down, to know his story would not be forgotten, brought him closure.

Just as I had become homeless, terrified, and full of despair, so had The Serb during World War II. It was the event that shaped his life. The years of starving, fighting, being put into concentration camps, escaping, only to be caught again haunted him as if they had happened yesterday.

I couldn't have written his story without having experienced my own "dark night of the soul". Each generation has its "war" to endure, the events that define it and make it strong. The Serbian gave me the courage to overcome my past and chase my dreams. The only thing I could give him back was his story and some companionship.

With Esah in school, The Serb and I had developed a ritual of going to the movies on Tuesday afternoons for "Two Dollar Tuesdays". It was always a challenge to find a movie with enough substance to keep The Serbian's interest. The fluffy stuff that generally populated the screens made him angry. He had always been frugal, and hated being ripped off.

One sunny afternoon we joined a flock of other white haired seniors and went to the new film in town, *The English Patient*. It was adapted from a book by a Canadian writer, Michael Ondaatje, and I was a huge fan. It was brought to life on film by Anthony Minghella. The Serb preferred foreign films and period pieces, so I felt this was a good bet.

I wheeled him into the theatre and parked him next to my aisle seat. The lights went down, and the opening music filled the darkened room. I was in heaven. Here, I could take a break from the demands of reality and revel in the art of the cinema. The opening shot was the most artistic I had seen in a long time. A single prop plane flew over the sand dunes of Africa near the close of WWII. I felt The Serbian sigh and relax next to me. He could feel the intention of the filmmaker, a fellow artist, and knew he was in for a great ride.

The film is about a man, burned beyond recognition, being tended by a French Canadian nurse near the close of the war. As she takes care of him, his story unfolds. He has lost the great love of his life, and is now dying in a bombed out building. In the final moments of the film, the nurse prepares a shot of morphine for her patient. He uses his burned claw of a hand to push all the morphine ampoules toward her, a silent plea to end his life.

I heard The Serbian sob next to me and I peered anxiously through the darkness at his shape huddled in the wheelchair. Tears were streaming down his face. He knew this man's pain. He knew the despair. One day, he would want the same merciful release.

20

A FILMMAKER IS BORN

Even though John and I could no longer live together, it was a blessing to spend time with him now that he was behaving like the man I met on Venice Beach. I wanted Esah to know what a great man his father could be. One Fourth of July, John and I took Esah to a local park to watch fireworks. As we walked through the grass, the afternoon sun casting long shadows in front of us, Esah wiggled in between us, taking us each by the hand. He jumped excitedly when he saw our shadows, a man and woman with their child in between.

"Look! We're a family!" he squealed. He had waited his whole life to be able to say that. It broke my heart.

I had spoken to counselors about John and they finally shed some light on his behavior pattern. They explained that abused children like John grow up thinking the world is a bad place. They equate love with abuse. If the world proves them wrong and is a wonderful place, they quickly do something to sabotage it. This keeps the outer world matching their inner bad world.

I realized that whenever things were going well for us, John would do something to sabotage it. When his meditation mandalas were selling for thousands of dollars and we had a waiting list for his drums, he would vanish. He even admitted to me once that he didn't believe I loved him unless I was yelling at him. So, naturally, he had to keep giving me reasons to get angry.

Now, something wonderful was happening for me, I was making a short film about his camp on Venice Beach. I didn't want John to superimpose his flawed vision of the world on it. When the time came to start filming, I knew I couldn't tell him in advance about it, or he would disappear, and I wanted him to experience this. For weeks I had been assembling a cast and crew, thanks to the San Diego Film Commission.

Many young filmmakers are fond of making their indie films "Gorilla Style", skulking through the streets without pulling permits, getting insurance, or feeding their volunteers. I knew I wanted to be legit. If I was to have any future in this industry, I wanted to learn how to do it right.

By registering the shoot with the San Diego Film Commission, over thirty-five people were referred to me and worked as free crew. Everyone who was looking for a film credit kept in touch with the film commission to see if any "student films" were being shot.

The commissioner gladly gave people my name, and we even ended up with seasoned crew who were between shoots, just looking for a film set to hang out on. It's addicting, being on set, and many people were happy to help out to be in that magic bubble again.

All of my actors were inexperienced young kids looking for their first break. I had found them in an acting class at the local college. I was touched to learn that every actor who wound up on my film had been homeless at some point. Some remembered sleeping in cars with their moms, others being alone on the street. They were the perfect cast because they all had heart and compassion. It made up for their inexperience.

We only had permits and insurance to film for four days, so I rehearsed the cast relentlessly as if we were doing a live stage play. The Serbian loved having creative souls in the house again. His large fishing van became our production vehicle. He would sit in his chair and laugh gleefully as we practiced the scenes.

One weekend I borrowed a video camera from my yoga group, and took everyone down to Mission Beach for a dress rehearsal. When we had completed filming we huddled around The Serb's television and played it back. It was horrible! But we had a good laugh and vowed not to make the same mistakes when the high priced equipment was rolling.

In Robert Rodriquez' book he mentioned that people making their first films can often get free film from the manufacturers, the key is to give them lots of warning. I had called Kodak in Los Angeles three months ahead of time and spoke to a marketing manager. She said she'd put my name on a box and toss in whatever came by. I phoned her back every month to nudge her memory. She had always forgotten about me, but was impressed with my persistence. Finally, it was time to pick up the film. I called her, she paused, then magic happened.

"We've launched a new film stock. Our reps just came off the trade show circuit with it. I have a bunch of 16 mm New Vision stock sitting here, you want it? All I ask is that your cinematographer give us a critique."

"Sure, that would be lovely." I carefully put the phone down and turned into a lunatic. I screamed, whooped, jumped up and down then ran a few laps around the back yard, scaring the crap out of the Serb. When I finally settled down I told him what had happened. He knew the importance of synchronicity in an artistic venture.

A gentle smile spread across his face. “Dat is good.”

A young man who needed a directing credit had gotten my name from the film commission and called me. He had been shadowing me for months, learning every nuance of the script. The plan was that he would direct the piece while I made lunches, ran errands, kept people off the set, and oh yeah, remembered to look after my kid. People asked why I didn’t want to direct. Honestly, after writing and rewriting the piece for months I was sick of it. I would be back at it in the editing process, and I liked the idea of a new, younger set of eyes on it.

When the day arrived to get the film from Kodak, my budding Director picked me up for the two hour drive Los Angeles. The entire trip north through San Diego County into L.A. was surreal. We kept looking at each other and bursting out laughing.

I played navigator and we found our way into the parking lot of Kodak. It was a massive complex. I had been told to come to the marketing building, so we parked out front. As we walked through the massive front doors we stepped out of the California heat into an icy vault. In hushed reverence we moved past Oscars encased in glass to the front reception. We were in one of Hollywood’s holy shrines, and almost afraid to talk.

The “Director of First Impressions” (that’s a receptionist for normal folks) buzzed my contact. She appeared around the corner with thousands of dollars worth of film in a box. Nonchalantly waving goodbye, as if this happened to us on a daily basis, we hustled the box out to the car and drove back down the coast. This was really going to happen. We were really going to make a movie. We drove in silence as the magnitude of the undertaking took hold.

My cinematographer was a friend from Vancouver. We used to talk and dream about making movies, and he had stayed in touch when I moved to L.A. I had written him after my adventure on Venice Beach years before. He had sent a desperate letter in return. He asked me if I ever stopped to think that maybe what I was doing was dangerous, that maybe I shouldn't act on every impulse that floated through my bizarre brain.

I invited him to come to Leucadia and meet John. He did and immediately fell in love with him. He videotaped John making a drum, and talked to him endlessly about life. His parting words were, "If you ever make your story into a film, I'll come down and do it for free."

It had been years and I hoped the offer was still good. It was. He would work for free but the camera he needed to rent would be pricey. I agreed.

He flew in two days before we were supposed to start filming. While he checked his gear at The Serb's house, I called the man who was supposed to provide our grip truck. His truck contained all the equipment ("expendables") I would need on set: clamps, sand bags to keep lights from blowing over in the wind, cables, you name it. A few weeks earlier he had promised to give us a great deal.

Apparently promises are farts in a wind storm when you're filmmaking. I called only to learn he had buggered off to Arkansas. A better job had landed in his unscrupulous lap. Did he think to call me so I could make other arrangements? Nope. No phone call, no sorry about that, just gone.

I told my cameraman the bad news. His news was even more exciting. The camera was dead. Batteries were dead, camera was dead, everything was dead. As my dreams collapsed around me in flames, I did the only logical thing possible, I went to bed. I told the cameraman to get some sleep. It was late; there was nothing we could do. Maybe everything would look better in the morning.

The next morning I meditated until the film commission office opened, then called my contact. I asked if we could postpone the shoot by one day while I put out fires. He said sure, as long as the insurance company would change the dates on our policy. I had a million dollar general liability insurance policy in case someone on set tripped on a cable and decided to sue me. The insurance company agreed to move the dates back, and I called back the film commissioner. He gave me the name of an "expendables" group who might be able to help me out. I called them and they instructed us to haul ass down to their warehouse in San Diego and they'd see what they could do.

The cameraman decided to try the camera one more time, Voila! It purred like a kitten. He couldn't believe it. I suggested maybe it had jet lag the night before. Whatever it was, our luck was changing. We jumped in the Serb's fishing van, er, our production vehicle, and tore down the freeway into San Diego. We found the "expendables" company and went inside. A wonderful gal at the front desk listened to our story.

"You're from Canada?" Yes. "From Calgary?" Yes. "Which high school?"

She had gone to the same high school and recognized my famous basketball playing brother's name. What are the odds? Even my cameraman was starting to look spooked. We had a deal.

I stopped being "The Producer" and became the roadie, loading equipment as fast as they threw it at me. When she handed me the bill, it was a fraction of the price the other grip truck would have cost. It was obvious Existence really wanted this film to happen.

Exhilarated, I was ready to drive home when the camera guy asked for one more stop. We drove around the industrial district to a warehouse. He ran in and returned with a giant piece of gold lamé and miles of tubing.

"What the hell do we need that for?" was my gracious response.

"Cuz you're special."

I didn't want to know. We roared home. The next day, instead of beginning filming, we had everyone over to the house to rehearse, with camera guy pretending to film and getting in everybody's face. Within an hour they were no longer jittery about the camera and relaxed into their roles. It was magical.

Finally, the day to begin filming arrived. As the cast and crew headed to Mission Beach in San Diego to film, I swung by the bakery that had offered me its day old pastries every day of the shoot. Despite being limited to an unheard of four days to film a half hour short, a magic bubble appeared around us and it was the most amazing four days of my life. Local restaurants that knew me had donated food to feed everyone, with enough left over to feed the homeless who came by to watch and chat with me about it. I remember encouraging one homie to take an extra muffin for later, we had lots.

"No, I want to make sure there's enough for my pal, Jimmy." The same homie rules applied here as in

Venice Beach, they always watched out for their friends, and didn't take more than they needed.

Over forty cast and crew showed up to work for free. The local film commissioner even came down to hang out. After juggling multi-million dollar projects, he loved the innocence of ours. He just stood there smiling day after day.

As the sun sailed high into the sky, so did our 10 foot square piece of gold lamé. It was a flamboyant sail announcing we were here, but more practically, it backlit the actors' faces so that they weren't completely whitewashed by the dazzling beach sun. Everyone had a wonderful golden glow about them, thanks to our lamé. Lesson learned.

As people hustled, crowds gathered, and I answered twenty questions a minute, Esah watched in awe. He finally crept up to me and tugged on my hand.

"Mom, are you the boss?"

We shared a moment of absolute awe and wonder. "Yeah, Honey, I'm the boss."

I had been transformed from a cleaning lady to a filmmaker in the blink of an eye. Our world was spinning on a magical axis.

On the final day of filming, I made a surprise visit to the shop where John was making signs for local businesses. I wanted him to be part of this. The final scene depicted John's character walking down the boardwalk into the night, holding the hand of the ghost of his son, played by our son, Esah. An actor was playing John, so I asked the real Rasta John if he would sit on the wall and drum.

He started to cry. "Thank you for giving me another chance, for telling my story, so people will know what happened."

At 2 a.m., the camera crew was ready. John smiled at me, a faint hint of his old self appeared. "I feel like Hitchcock, making a cameo in my own film."

He sat on the beach wall, in the dark, and drummed his heart out, as his son walked by into the night.

*****

It was one of the last times we would see John. He began having Grand Mal seizures, the result of a brain tumor. The first one happened on Main Street in Encinitas. People who witnessed it said his dreadlocks saved him because he fell straight backwards on to the sidewalk.

His hero, Bob Marley, had died of a brain tumor. So had John's mother, despondent about the reality of being black in America. John refused to undergo the same torture he'd witnessed his mother go through, so he walked away from the hospital after the first seizure.

I don't know how long someone can survive, homeless with a brain tumor. When John walked away from the hospital, he vanished from our lives forever. He has been missing, presumed dead, for over fifteen years. Thankfully, his greatest work of art lives on in his son.

As he was disappearing from our lives, so was The Serbian. His health was steadily deteriorating. I was woken up at all hours of the night by the frantic ringing of his bedside bell. I did the best I could, but lifting him, single-handedly, out of bed and carrying him to the bathroom was hard on both of us.

One night, after a particularly trying episode, he lay in bed crying and apologizing for being such a burden. Trying to save face for both us of us, I told him that after he went back to sleep those nights I was having the best midnight meditations ever. We both laughed, until we started crying again. But it was true. After I returned The Serbian to bed I would sit out back staring at the moon, and feel an absolute, unwavering connection with Existence.

It became obvious that the Serb needed round the clock nursing, and not a round the clock writer. Esah, Rainbow Kitty, and I were on the move again. In the nine years I had been in California, I had moved 35 times. We were urban nomads.

My yoga teacher in Encinitas was connected to an artist's colony called "The Loft" in San Diego. He told me it had inexpensive studios we could live in(sounds good), a yoga room (better), a computer software company willing to give me a job (yessss) and post production studios where I could finally edit my film! I was breathless! It was too good to be true. My camera man had taken our film back to Vancouver, British Columbia, to have it developed and color corrected. But I was out of money and needed to find cheap post-production facilities where I could edit it. This looked like my ticket.

The Serb, in his final magnanimous gesture, allowed us to borrow the van to move. The day we left was the most painful exit I'd made to date. Years of renting rooms with families and becoming attached to the kids had made me pretty thick skinned about leaving. But this was something else, like a memory from a past life, a loved one I had left before.

The Serbian sat by the front door in his wheelchair, silently watching me load up the van. When we were ready to go I stood before him. His small fragile form barely filled his wheelchair. I couldn't speak. He reached out and grabbed my hand. The strength of his grip shocked me. His eyes bored into my soul.

"Don't go" they said.

I felt like I was abandoning him, but there was nothing I could do. And like the children I had left behind at so many other homes, I kissed him goodbye and walked out the door.

21

THE LOFT

"The Loft" was a beautiful old building in downtown San Diego. It was within walking distance of cozy art galleries, outdoor cafes, and Horton Plaza. The ocean glimmered in the distance. Despite being in bad need of repair, the building had real charm. Every eight by twelve artist's loft had a twelve foot high ceiling, floor to ceiling window, and hardwood floors. The ornate work on the façade of the building would probably qualify it as a historic site once it was restored. This was what the owner was banking on. In exchange for cheap rent, all of the tenants were required to do cleaning, maintenance, as well as construction on Saturdays, turning more of the open warehouse space into rental loft studios.

The building manager was a rare, exotic bird I fondly nicknamed, "The Dungeon Master". He was considered "The Dark One" by the Yoga group, and he only came out at night. He was an orphan who had grown up to be a nearsighted, twenty-something, computer geek with his hand in more deals than you could wave your incense stick at.

He wanted nothing to do with the yoga group who made up half of the building's tenants. He rented the rest of the studio lofts to starving musicians, artists, strippers, and fellow IT geeks. When I arrived with my cat and my kid I could hear him sharpening his Dungeons and Dragons broadsword.

A boutique software company had offices, and studios, on the second floor. They hired me to market and bundle their products. I had ten years of marketing and advertising experience from Canada, and figured I could do this with my eyes closed. They agreed to pay me a minimum salary, plus rent, and allow me to edit my film in their *Adobe Premier* editing suite.

The company wanted their name on my lease since they were paying the rent. The Dungeon Master refused; the room would be in my name. I was in his realm and under his control. I didn't know this small technicality would keep us from becoming homeless again before the year was out.

And so we moved up to our loft on the fourth floor. It's such an easy thing to write, "we moved in", but the reality was we had to park The Serb's van around the corner from The Loft, hustle our stuff around the block, through the massive locked steal front door and into the urine stained lobby. The elevator was a gaping hole in the middle of the building (note to self, keep six year old away from hole) so we walked our belongings up four flights to the top.

The Loft residents were used to the sweaty migration of new tenants. Any resident who walked by an abandoned pile of stuff at one of the landings would grab an armful and walk it up to the next one. Through this communal effort, we finally had a pile of boxes and clothes on the top floor. The lofts on the third floor were all finished, complete with varnished hardwood floors and exotic décor. It was also the floor the art studio and yoga rooms were on.

Our room was on the fourth floor and only the second to be framed and dry walled up there. The rest of the space was a huge expanse of dangling wires, exposed pipes, and holes in the floor. Esah was afraid of this wasteland, and I couldn't blame him. Good thing we brought a mouser with us; Rainbow Kitty immediately earned her keep by becoming the scourge of all the resident rodents and cockroaches.

The greatest treasure at The Loft was "Mama". She was an elegant, eighty year old Southern Belle who had the studio on the top floor next to us. She made the decision that as an octogenarian she would rather throw her money in with a yoga group than retire into a senior's resident. She never regretted the decision. She was the heart of the building. Most mornings found her in the kitchen, making home made bread, having tea, and lending an ear, or shoulder to cry on, to any waif who came by. Her Thanksgiving open house was legendary, often feeding over a hundred wayward and homeless teens.

Her daily routine never varied. At 6 a.m. she would shuffle across the huge undeveloped expanse from her room to the breakfast nook. After tea and toast she would walk up Broadway to a hotel that gave her swimming privileges in their pool. She would swim for a leisurely hour; pick up her groceries for the day, then walk up the four flights of stairs to her room.

And here I was practically passing out from exhaustion after floundering up the stairs. When Esah and I finally dropped the last of our load in our room, Mama was our Welcome Wagon. She was thrilled to have neighbors on her floor. Esah was the only child in the building. Her grandchildren lived back east so she turned all of her grandmother energy on him. She graciously invited us into her place to relax while she made tea. Her hardwood floor was afloat in turquoise tinted varnish, giving it the appearance of a blue sea. Antiques nested on every surface. Floor gnomes and unicorns peeked out from behind giant potted palms.

Mama was grace incarnate. She offered us refreshments in her lovely, lilting Southern accent, and cradled us in her nest, softening the blow of yet another move. We were lucky enough to have the kitchen and giant screen TV on our floor. Mama shuffled away to fetch tea and biscuits, allowing me to doze, while Esah played *Lego* in front of her large corner windows facing Broadway.

Before we could unpack a thing The Dungeon Master stalked in and announced we had to make ourselves scarce, there was a Rave Party on our floor that night. It was one of the many illicit revenue streams The Dungeon Master orchestrated.

He offered to let us stay in a room one floor down for the night to get away from the party. We followed him downstairs to a beautiful room decorated in an oriental style; a large Bronze Buddha sat on a mahogany chest at one end. This was the guest room for visiting yoga teachers. I was thrilled. He smirked and walked away.

There was excitement in the air as the various Loft dwellers crept out of their hiding places and watched the decorating going on upstairs. We soon met our neighbors; the stripper, the trumpet player, the handyman (and master of cartoon voices), and assorted computer geeks with bottle thick specs. There was even a Marine. I was by far the oldest person in the place (excluding Mama). They weren't that different from the homies of Venice Beach, and I knew if I just "behaved" and helped out, they would eventually let me join their "camp".

It didn't take long. Esah, at six years of age, could soften anyone's heart. These outcasts responded to his innocence. Most of them were alone, or runaways, and missed the company of an untainted soul; someone who woke up with a big smile, eager to see what the day would bring.

He loved climbing things and as we watched the decorating committee do its magic, Esah spotted a plumbing pipe traveling through the middle of the space. In no time, he had shimmied up it and touched the ceiling. He came back down to a round of applause and was soon zooming through the building, playing *Mortal Combat* with none other than our resident stripper.

She had a full sleeve tat (tattoo covering her entire arm) of yoga symbols including lotus flowers, cobras, Hindu gods, and "Om". That combined with her flaming red hair made her quite a vision. She had taken on the name "Garuda" after the Hindu God, which intimidated most of the guys.

But Esah saw through her fierce disguise. She was a runaway who had been stripping since she was fourteen. She was thrilled to be a kid again with my son. Every guy in the place would have given his soul to play with her, but Esah won. I promised Esah we would stay and watch a bit of the Rave, but then we had to go downstairs to bed.

The Dungeon Master had done a remarkable job of transforming the open space for the event. A huge nine by twelve foot video screen covered one wall and was soon playing Japanese Anime films to the mind blowing sound system he had installed. Loud Techno Disco music bounced off the walls and windows, as the young kids started to drift in. I signaled Esah and we hustled downstairs - to our room - that was directly beneath the bass bins upstairs.

Rainbow Kitty was hiding under the bed, little kitty paws pressed hard against her ears trying to drown out the noise. We stared at each other in horror as the bed bounced, the walls shook, sleep a wayward wish.

"What the hell have I gotten us into this time?" I thought, close to tears. "OMMM!!" I chanted, trying to ignore the booming upstairs.

"OM!!" giggled Esah, covering his ears and grinning at me.

"OOOMMMM!!" We screamed as loud as we could, barely hearing ourselves above the throbbing in my solar plexus. Resistance was futile. A loud rumbling began.

"What's that new noise?" I yelled.

Layered over the rock concert din was something resembling a train. Esah shrugged and curled up with the cat. They both fell asleep - unbelievable. My brains were rattling too hard to sleep.

I went back upstairs to get a clear picture of the Apocalypse. Ah, roller skates. That was the new sound. A sea of raging teen hormones bounced in the centre of the room, while others roller skated around the perimeter. It was actually more bearable being at the party, than under it, so I stayed. The Dungeon Master had several girls selling water. Young kids with sparkles in their hair, *Winnie the Pooh* backpacks, and cartoon paraphernalia were dancing, laughing, and having a non-drug-induced high. I was impressed.

By 6 a.m. they were still hard at it. Even at the height of my wild times, I rarely stayed up all night. I saw The Dungeon Master pushing people around at the far edge of the gathering; parting the Red Sea of Riff Raff , making way for Mama. She shuffled across the dance floor in her pink floral dressing gown, pink fuzzy slippers, tea pot in hand. It was time for her breakfast.

Partiers witnessing this vision probably thought

they were hallucinating. The granny smiled and nodded as she passed, her bodyguard (The Dungeon Master) manhandling anyone who didn't clear the way fast enough. Who knew? Maybe he had some redeeming qualities after all. I later found out that Mama was the closest thing he had ever had to family, and he would have killed for her.

As the Rave finally fizzled to an exhausted end, The Dungeon Master spotted me. He thrust a garbage bag in my hand and told me to start cleaning up. I wasn't sure this was part of the deal I had agreed to, but I did what I was told, hoping it would cut me some slack from this guy. I heard him go downstairs and start banging on doors, dragging people out of their nests, turning our peaceful Sunday into a forced labor camp. We moved like zombies, cleaning the debris, stumbling over lovely little nooks of vomit. The bathroom was nightmarish: one toilet for two hundred kids simply didn't cut it.

I heard one of the young musicians gag and stumble away from a room that had just been dry walled and was ready for painting. We all went over to look. Someone had taken a dump in the middle of the floor. The males fled the scene at the sight of human feces.

Lord knows I'd changed enough diapers and bathtubs full of poop submarines. This seemed to have my name all over it. I grabbed a shovel and went in. I didn't even request a gas mask. The Dungeon Master was impressed.

As I shoveled the mess up and cleaned and disinfected the room, I heard him bragging. "Yeah, real tough guys, the mom had to clean it up. What a bunch of pussies!" I was his hero, or did this make me his bitch?

It took a while to adjust to this new chaos. Late at night, with no light burning except our little bedside lamps, Esah had to take the flashlight and cat and pick his way through the construction zone to get to the bathroom. It was a scary trek by anyone's standards. I told him to pretend he was in the video game *Mortal Combat* and turn it into a game.

Years later we were visiting friends back in Canada and their sons were afraid to go downstairs to their fully developed Rumpus Room because the light was off. Esah, much younger and smaller than these boys, grabbed a fake sword and stepped into the darkness. "Don't worry, I'll protect you."

As the philosopher Horace once said, "*Adversity reveals genius, prosperity conceals it.*"

When September rolled around it was time for Esah to begin Grade One. The school division had a home schooling option that would keep Esah with me instead of the tough downtown school which made me nervous to say the least.

We registered and were assigned a lovely, artistic man who would become our counselor. He was at my beck and call to answer any and all questions I had about teaching my son. He explained to me that the joy of home schooling was it could be done anywhere. If we did math equations at the beach in the sand, I could take a picture and send it in to him. If Esah watched a great show on the Discovery Channel, he could write a paragraph about it and send it in. Our counselor had students that were traveling around the world with their parents, mailing projects in from exotic locales. It was a perfect fit.

*****

The intensity of living in the downtown core was offset by the weekends at "The Land" (these guys weren't big on fancy titles). It was a yoga retreat in the high desert where everyone practiced sunrise yoga, meditated, did seva (meaning being of service), read various spiritual teachings, and communed with nature.

To get there we drove east out of San Diego for hours, then south to a piece of land butting up against the Mexican border. Once on the property we drove down a narrow dirt road past massive boulders littering the landscape. This was the high desert, cold enough for snow during the winter and intense heat during the summer.

The main yoga building slowly appeared over the boulders as we drove down the hill for the first time. Two enormous Tibetan eyes peered at us. The entire side of the main yoga/eating quarters was painted with a massive Tibetan face. The building had originally been a small cabin with a kitchen, bathroom and living room downstairs. Over time the yoga group had extended the living room to connect to a yoga studio with hardwood floors and floor to ceiling windows. It was breathtaking to look out those windows, taking in the beautiful desert landscape and sunrises. A ladder led upstairs to the sleeping area full of teal green futon mattresses. We were woken up every morning at 4:30 am by the gentle ringing of a bell to lead us downstairs for Sunrise yoga practice.

The retreat was used to teach many different spiritual practices. As a result, different meditation caves in the area were painted and decorated in beautiful, unique styles. One was full of crystals, another held a statue of the Virgin Mary, yet another contained huge Turkish thrones and Sufi paintings.

One of the most interesting yoga poses I learned out there was a Kundalini Yoga practice taught by Yogi Bhajan called “Sat Kriya”. We sat on our heels (that took some doing, I had to start off with lots of pillows under my butt) and held our arms straight over our head. My elbows were kept tight against my ears, hands clasped, index fingers pointing sky ward. As we chanted “Sat Nam” (*Truth is my Identity* in Sanskrit) we pumped air out of our diaphragm by pumping our stomachs in and out. It took some doing, but was aimed at strengthening the nerves, especially after an emotional blow.

Apparently when the teachings were first brought to America, some students had to do this pose for months to undo the damage that drugs, especially marijuana, had done to their systems. It was the reason drug addicts had trouble with life even after they had stopped using. Their nerves were shot. Considering the fragile state of my nerves, this pose became my favorite.

Being out at the yoga retreat got me thinking about our pet. Downtown living really wasn’t her thing. Talks with the retreat staff revealed that giant kangaroo mice (yup, mice that hop like kangaroos) were chewing the electrical wires. They needed a mouser. I had a mouser. It was a match made in heaven. We moved her out to the Land.

Normally we slept in the upstairs loft above the yoga studio, but Rainbow Kitty couldn’t get up there so they let us take over the teepee that was on the property. Esah was part Blackfoot, so the only legitimate heir to the dwelling anyway. It suited Rainbow Kitty just fine. She could move freely in and out of the teepee all night while doing her hunting. When I tried to bring more cat food out to the Land they told me not to bother, she was getting fat off mice.

Esah loved it out there just as much. He could run wild like, well, like the Dog Boy of Leucadia. We'd soak in the hot tub late at night, staring at the star spangled heavens, and for a brief moment in time be suspended in a state of grace.

In exchange for being "Staff", Esah and I could be out there every weekend. One weekend a Dena woman held a traditional Sweat Lodge ceremony. She taught us to pick certain herbs for use in special salt rubs and teas. Next we formed a sweat lodge from tree branches covered with red clay. While we were waiting for our sweat lodge to dry for our evening sweat we decided to go for a stroll. Esah chased butterflies and explored ahead of us on the trail.

We came around a corner and were confronted with the most amazing sight. Where there had once been a pond, there was now a huge sea of mud, filled with thousands of dying cat fish. Massive blue herons stood in the mud leisurely feasting on the dying fish.

Esah was distraught, "We have to save them!"

I tried to take a step into the pond, and immediately sunk up to my knees in the deceptively deep muck. Esah, light as a feather, was fine, skimming across the surface with ease. As he sailed across the mud in the sunlight ahead of me, I flashed on his dad moving ahead of me that first night with him on Venice Beach.

Esah stopped about ten feet from shore and reached down for a fish. He gently scooped it up in his hands and ran back to us. "What should I do?"

"Let's take it back and get a bucket of water!"

He ran back down the path, with us in hot pursuit,

really hot, it was about 120 degrees out. He ran the full mile and a half back to the retreat. Esah found a bucket, filled it with water, and carefully placed the catfish in it.

The fish lazily swam around, as if it was no big deal to be abducted by an alien and carried in a hot sweaty hand to a virtual oasis of cool water. Apparently catfish can survive long droughts by burying themselves in the mud.

One of the oddities of the Land, and trust me there were many, was a water spigot in the middle of nowhere, with an old bath tub next to it. Esah quickly filled the bath tub with water, tossed the fish in, and headed back with his bucket for more. It took him the entire afternoon, but eventually, the bathtub was full of mud, algae, fish, and water. As the retreat guests came over to admire it, our Dine hostess made a sign out of an old piece of barn wood and stuck it next to the tub.

“Esah’s Sacred Catfish Pond”

That night, the women sat outside of the sweat lodge and drummed, while the men went inside, sweated, and hopefully solved the problems of the world. Esah, being a child, had to follow the native tradition and stay with the women.

The Native American drums were about 14” in diameter, and only 3” deep, covered in cow hide. We held them up and beat them with hide covered mallets. Esah was thrilled to be included, drumming around the bonfire, watching shooting stars, and listening to the coyotes howl in the distance.

When the men were done, instead of taking their turn around the fire and drumming for us, they all bolted for the cold pools up by the lodge. Wimps. It looked like we were on our own; our sweat would have to be done without any accompaniment.

I told Esah he might as well go to the pools with the other guys. One by one we entered the sweat lodge and covered the opening with deer skin. As we sat around the fire pit, beads of perspiration popping up on our skin, the sound of a lone drum filled the air. Esah, empowered by rescuing the catfish, decided he would be our man. We said prayers, gave thanks, and sweated bullets.

Esah later admitted he was scared to death, but thought it was mean that the other guys left us. So he did it alone. His journey as a spiritual warrior had begun.

*****

While weekends at the Land brought me immense peace, the situation at the Loft became stranger and stranger. Contradictions and hypocrisy became the order of the day. And I wasn't the only one caught off guard. Some other friends who had joined about the same time were starting to feel all was not well.

The leader of the group would go on massive, extravagant spending sprees, then announce to the group that we all had to pay for it. I was struggling to understand if this was some type of spiritual technique, or bullshit. The latter proved to be the case when a visiting Buddhist Monk was out at The Land holding a course. I heard him comment, "What's he going to want next, a jet?" Realizing other people in the spiritual community were not impressed with our "guru", I went on high alert.

I was working round the clock for this group, and had nothing to show for it. By Christmas we were penniless. Christmas morning was devastating. I had to explain to Esah why there were no presents.

It wasn't because he had been "naughty". He had, in fact, been the best kid imaginable. Santa was a hoax, the lack of presents was all my fault.

He put on a brave face and we went out for a morning stroll. I wanted to get as far away from The Loft as possible on this dismal morning. That's when the true spirit of Christmas revealed itself. All the homeless Vietnam Vets we had made friends with had something for Esah. Many had gone dumpster diving to find a toy they could clean up for him. Some had made primitive contraptions using scraps and ingenuity. The gift for them was that they had a child in their lives. One by one these lost men hugged Esah and wished him Merry Christmas.

As we huddled in our room that night, one of the yoga teachers came by and took Esah by the hand. "Come on, let's go see if anyone in the building has chores you could do to earn some money of your own."

The first stop was at the book worm's room. He paid Esah a dollar to dust his books with a tissue. Next, The Dungeon Master gave Esah ten dollars to clean his shoes with a tissue. One by one, residents in the building found a munchkin size job for him to do. By the time Esah came back to our room, he had made seventeen dollars. It was exactly the amount needed to buy the Lego set he'd been hoping for.

When I look back, it was probably the most empowering Christmas we could have had. Esah learned that he had the ability to create his own reality. I was reminded what the spirit of Christmas was really about, and that Existence still had my back.

As New Year's Eve approached, there were whispers of massive party plans, a party on every floor. One floor was even planning a Voodoo ritual. Great, perfect for a six year old.

My favorite New Year's Eve had been the one spent meditating at the *SRF* temple. I yearned for that type of peace and solace to ring in the New Year, rather than a potpourri of partiers trying to lose their minds. The caretaker from the Land happened to be in town one day, and I asked him if there was a chance of spending the holiday out there. He was thrilled; he didn't want to be alone, and loved Esah. We were set.

One other member of the troop was hoping for a quieter celebration as well and offered to drive us. We stopped on the way to buy provisions and arrived at the yoga retreat close to sunset. With the building empty, we opted to put our sleeping bags in the living room by the fireplace, rather than upstairs in the cold loft. When eleven o'clock rolled around, my two companions were sound asleep, so I headed out to the meditation caves alone.

One of the caves was an amazing structure created as a result of huge boulders rolling together over time. Inside, there was a worn, flat stone that had been used by Native Americans for centuries as a healing stone. Documentaries had been done on the otherworldly blue lights that had been witnessed shooting through the cave. One wandering Saddhu from Paramahamsa Yogananda's lineage had even called it a "Babaji" Cave.

I decided this was my spot. I reverently left my sandals outside and padded through the soft sand to the healing stone in the dark. I looked out the mouth of the cave at the night sky. Being so far from civilization afforded me a spectacular view of the Milky Way.

I said a prayer of thanks. Esah and I were going to make it. A meteorite shower sailed overhead and into Mexico. Coyotes howled in the distance. One meteorite seemed to be following the rest until it stopped, paused, then shot back the other way. I hoped whatever alien was on board was having as great a New Year's as I was. I sank into a deep meditation, and all of my cares vanished.

I was jolted out of my reverie by the sound of gunfire coming from across the border. It must be midnight. I smiled at the stars and thanked them for this night. I could see the soft lights glowing through the windows of the cabin and made my way back.

When we returned to the artist colony in San Diego, my new-found serenity was immediately tested. The place had been trashed by the partiers. Some were still there, curled up in fetal positions in corners. Lord knows what had transpired that night.

The software company, with the yoga "guru" in attendance, called a New Year's Day meeting. I was told I was no longer being paid for working for the software company; the money was going to the good of "The Group". Oh, and by the way, they told me that Esah was no longer mine, that he belonged to "The Group" as well. Obviously it was time to get back in my spaceship and return to the planet Crazy Pants.

I don't remember the exact words, or who said what first, but I told them what I thought of their scheme. The meeting ended with a large plate of food being thrown at my head. Esah appeared out of nowhere and yelled at the towering six foot tall red headed leader.

"Quit yelling at my mom!"

This humbled most of the group and they quickly disbanded. These tactics had probably worked for them with other recruits, but I don't think they had ever tackled a single Canadian mountain mom before. This man, this spiritual leader, was a con man. He had found a way to keep people enslaved, and paying for his lavish lifestyle, by promising them enlightenment and ultimately salvation.

My heart was racing as I realized I had stumbled into a Cult. Just when I thought the universe had nothing left to throw at me after the last ten years, here came the kitchen sink. I had always been disdainful of people who joined cults; sure I would never be that stupid. Now I knew how sinister the recruitment could be.

They had lured me there with the promise of fulfilling all my needs. They thought they had isolated me from any family. After all, mine was in Canada. When it looked like I had no means of escape, they finally showed me the fine print on their imaginary contract. I would have no money of my own, and be at their beck and call for life. My child would be held as collateral.

That night my Kriya Yoga meditation had a new desperation to it. How was I going to get us out of this? "Be still" was my answer. Suddenly there was a loud pounding on the door. Two men were demanding I come downstairs for another meeting. I looked at the small picture on my table of Paramahamsa Yogananda, his last smile before he left his body. "Hold your pose", he said.

The tirade outside the door grew louder. They kicked the wall where Esah was sleeping. Miraculously, or more accurately, as always, he slept through it. I had learned that when my lessons were in full swing, he was kept blissfully unaware and safe.

They tried to come in through the connecting door between my room and my neighbor, but luckily I had stored a large shipping trunk in front of it. I don't know where the others in the building were, but for over an hour these bouncers tried to bully me into coming to their meeting. Finally, they were almost whimpering.

"Please, just come downstairs. He's gonna keep sending people until you come."

I relented and left my room. As we walked to the stairs I saw The Dungeon Master hovering in the shadows. Amazingly, he was watching out for us. The Universe was prepared to send in bodyguards to help me if needed. I went to the boardroom of the software company for the final show down. The room oozed with menace as the surreal meeting began. They passed a paper to me, the equivalent of a contract. I was told to sign. I refused.

Their leader gave me a serpentine smile and suggested that if I didn't sign, I would no longer belong to "the group".

I slid it back to him. "That's the whole idea. You quit paying me. I'm filing for Unemployment."

The towering inferno of a "spiritual leader" rose up and stood nose to nose with me, screaming. All my life I had cowered in front of raging, angry men. I hated confrontation, especially if it was illogical. I would usually endure their rage, my insides twisting and turning. Stifling my emotions had led to years of back pain and varied illnesses.

But this life lesson was coming to an end. My nights of meditation, and first awkward attempts at standing up for myself, paid off. Instead of feeling I was standing up to a tropical storm, I felt a gentle breeze blowing by my face. I couldn't help myself, in the middle of his tirade, a huge smile spread over my face. The panic button that had been pushed my whole life had finally been disconnected. I was done. And he knew it. His mouth clanged shut. The group watched in disbelief as I turned and left the room.

They followed me into the main area like a lynch mob when a guardian angel appeared out of nowhere.

"Hey Meg, you need a hand moving your stuff?"

It was the computer IT guy who was installing a network for the software company. He was a roving boy genius who traveled the world. He had hair to his waist, looked about twenty-one, and had come to see what all the yelling was about. Just when I thought I was once again battling alone, two of society's misfits, The Dungeon Master and an IT genius, were ready to be knights in shining armor.

The IT guy was untouchable, and the cult knew it. If they pissed him off, they could kiss their computer network goodbye. He helped me clear my belongings out of the office and we disappeared upstairs to my studio, leaving the group seething behind us.

I checked on Esah. He was still blissfully asleep. IT Guy and I sat up and talked until sunrise. We talked about life, relationships, and how funny life could be. Last I heard from him was an e-mail from a catamaran in Belize. He was running his laptop off a car battery connected to a solar panel. Those are the kind of unique souls that kept me going, that kept the journey worth taking.

As I watched the sun rise on a new day, the Cult was planning my punishment for defying them. They needed to make an example of me so that other Cult members wouldn't leave. They tried to storm The Dungeon Master's domain and demand I be evicted. But the Dungeon Master was impossible to reach unless he wanted you to reach him. They left messages on his cell phone until the mail box exploded and slipped messages under the door of his room, to no avail.

Finally, he met with them, and he was ready. He had seen it all before. He'd watched them railroad people into their "Group" then take every penny they had. He realized as he got to know me that I didn't know what I'd gotten myself into.

They demanded he throw me out of my room. It was their room after all. The Dungeon Master showed them the rental agreement and reminded them the room was in my name. They smugly retreated, knowing that when rent came due at the first of the month, I would be homeless.

The safety net known as Existence was ready. Right on cue, my income tax refund appeared. I was probably the only one in the building doing legal paperwork for anything. I took the refund, cashed it, and paid The Dungeon Master for the next month's rent. We became co-conspirators.

The Cult lost its hypocritical mind. Esah and I continued to greet them in the hall with big smiles and cheery greetings. They scurried past like rats, scowling and being very unenlightened. Now that I was unemployed, The Dungeon Master made me a business proposition. He needed someone he could trust to sell the tickets for the Raves, was I interested?

Why not? It was obvious normal solutions for earning a living weren't possible for me anymore. We had a deal. The night of the Rave, he walked me across town to an underground record store where the tickets would be sold. He explained that the location had to be kept secret until the night of the party. Kids would call his message machine which had a recorded message giving my location.

They would come to me at the record store, buy their tickets and I would give them their next "clue". It was a giant scavenger hunt. Eventually they would wind up at The Loft and partying would ensue. Within the space of a few hours, I sold thousands of dollars worth of tickets, then walked through the dark streets alone back home.

One week it was a hip hop party with black bouncers the size of buildings. Another week it was a *Labyrinth* party with the David Bowie movie *Labyrinth* playing on the big screen while kids dressed in velvet jackets and flowing gowns danced in the newly painted white warehouse space.

Esah and I enjoyed quiet peaceful days once again. I didn't have a clue what direction we would be flung in next. Then, one Sunday morning as I was meditating, I realized I was done. I had met the last California nut case I needed to meet. We hadn't been able to find John, and I was tired of waiting for something that may never happen. I wanted Esah to grow up with sane people who had his best interest at heart. It was time to go back to Canada.

I borrowed Mama's phone and called my parents. I told them it was over, I was coming home. I had been gone for ten years on an adventure that was supposed to last a month.

My dad broke down. He was much older than mom, and his health was failing. He often said to me during our weekly phone calls that he didn't know why he was still around, he had done everything he wanted to do, and he was ready to go.

After that phone call, it became clear he was waiting for me to come home. Mom said he had a burst of energy that lasted several days. They visited friends, he won at bridge night, and they visited our old home that he had so lovingly renovated every year for the thirty years they had lived in it. After walking around the old neighborhood, he passed away on the sidewalk by our old house.

Our neighbors rallied around mom and made all the necessary phone calls and arrangements. It was over, the end of an era, and I was coming home. Within forty-eight hours I had booked a flight, and given away our things to the lost souls in the Loft. During the ten years I had been in California, I had lived in thirty-six places. For the sake of my son, it was time to set down roots and give him a real home.

The night before our flight I said a prayer for John. We would never know what happened to him, or why his remains were never found. But when I slept, I dreamt of a lone, broken man with dreadlocks walking into the ocean, letting it take him home.

PART THREE:

INDIA

22

THE AVATAR

"The wound is the place where the Light enters you"
– Rumi

I sat on the front steps of the open air granite temple in the predawn light of South India. Across the courtyard bonfires were burning, preparing the coals for the sacred Panchas Tapas meditation for peace. I stared into the black granite eyes of Nandi, the temple bull. There was comfort in this huge stone beast. I guess that's why he was eternally guarding the temple.

The sun began to hint at making an appearance behind the majestic Royal Palms facing me. I couldn't sleep that first night at the ashram in India after twenty-six hours on a plane, so I decided to wander around the sacred space while I had it to myself.

It's hard to describe how light-headed I felt, how miraculous the whole trip was. After nineteen years of raising my son alone, stressing over every bill, every 'what if?' the pressure had inexplicably and completely left as I walked the ashram grounds.

After leaving California I had continued my Kriya Yoga practice while living the working life. Every morning I meditated and did yoga. I found that it set the rules for the day. By telling the Universe "We're going to do it MY way", I limited the number of assholes who could mess with my reality. Any day I missed my morning practice, I paid the price for it with all manner of things going wrong.

I knew I was supposed to stay put to give my son the secure start in life he deserved. The days of being a nomad were on hold. There were times, in the middle of the night, when I wondered if this was really all there was? After my huge adventure in California, was I really just deep down one of the working poor? None of my writing projects took flight. I continued to write down the screenplays that played in my head, but no one could get them made. As a matter of fact, anyone who tried to produce my work went out of business or lost their jobs. I was the "Typhoid Mary" of screenwriting apparently.

I was going to stop writing all together, then realized how much comfort it brought me, to write in the night while my child slept. It had become my entertainment. So, I began calling it a hobby instead of a goal, and carried on, the scripts piling up under my bed like so many dust bunnies.

Esah continued to meditate as well, developing his own quiet practice quite separate from mine. I'm not sure what his technique was, but it kept him balanced and made him a joy to be around. He never became a dreaded teenager. Instead he helped with chores, made me laugh, and reminded me not to be so serious. He graduated from high school with honors, then worked for a year saving up to travel. On July 4th, America's Independence Day, I drove him to the Calgary airport for his first solo trip.

He was planning on walking and camping his way through Central and South America. We stood looking at each other in wonder at the Departures

Gate. My smile was full of amazement that I had done it, raised a whole human being, and he didn't need me anymore. His was one of nervous excitement, not sure what he was doing, but convinced he had to do it.

"See ya", I said.

"See ya", he replied, and was gone.

There was nothing left to say. The massive adventure was complete, and now he was off to find out who he really was. I stared out the window at his flight until it disappeared into the clear blue, and drove myself home to our tiny basement walk out apartment.

"So, now what are you going to do?" asked the Voice.

"I don't know", I thought.

My reasons for keeping a roof over my head were gone. Two days later I received a call from India. Paramahamsa Nithyananda had heard about the way I was interpreting his teachings in Canada and wanted me to write for him. He was the newest incarnation in the lineage of my first guru, Paramahamsa Yogananda, and I had been following his teachings and techniques for the past two years.

"How soon can you get here?" his people asked.

"Er, tomorrow?"

*****

I closed my eyes and swam in the most beautiful meditation space imaginable. Gradually people began wandering up the hill to the temple for the meditation. I was wearing summer clothes from Canada, but they were already too heavy for the warm India morning. I was going to have to do some shopping for traditional Indian outfits to survive the heat.

I sat on the platform facing the spot the young Avatar would take. I could hear people taking their seats around me, birds began singing, the bonfires crackled, and I went into another dimension.

Suddenly a jolt of electricity, like a lightning bolt, shot through my entire system. My eyes flew open to see Nithyananda facing me a few meters away in deep mediation. He was sitting in a circle of red hot coals, burning away the negativity of the world.

“Welcome home”, said the Voice.

Later, when Nithyananda walked by, he gently put his hand on my head in blessing. I felt the energy shooting between us.

“I am with you,” he said.

And I knew he was. This was the Cosmic connection I had been searching for my whole life. I was finally experiencing the quantum physics behind my spiritual beliefs. Here was a soul that was physically changing the game I was playing. I could feel the electricity flowing through me in a way I had never experienced in my life. That’s when I began relating to him as my Swamiji, a term of endearment for one’s guru.

*****

One morning we were sitting in one of Nithyananda’s large lecture halls, being put through another soul searching, healing process. He started us off with the statement, “Life is hopeless. Find the nearest trash bin and just throw yourself inside.”

Many people found this sentence so absurd they burst out laughing. I, on the other hand, felt my Being shatter. All the pain and hardship of being an only parent and constantly trying to believe there was hope flooded my soul. The anguish and solitude that had filled my years as a mom surged through me. I was finally being given permission to let go and admit life is hopeless. I knew I couldn't be that person anymore. I wanted to feel true joy again. That knock your socks off, can't stop laughing kind of joy I knew as a child.

I mentally found a dumpster and threw myself in it. I pictured myself in a back alley in Venice Beach, staring up at the stars. I cried for all the years of pain and loneliness. I cried for all the shattered dreams. And then I felt peace.

"Just stop," Swamiji instructed.

And I did. I had found a teacher who could take the pain, and handle it for me. By surrendering to the power and wisdom of Existence, through its representative, Paramahamsa Nithyananda, I was at peace.

An Avatar is a human being who wins the game, allowing the Divine energy to descend completely into their body without interference by ego. Being raised as a Christian, I was led to believe this only happened once, in Jesus. And we were all waiting with baited breath for that guy to show up again in the Second Coming of Christ. The fact is the second coming the Cosmos is waiting for is us. Each of us is supposed to rise to that consciousness.

As Jesus said, "All these things I do, so can you."

The more I was in the presence of this man, the more I realized this was an Avatar, and he was showing us all how to attain that state.

*****

The young Avatar touched my head and quietly moved away. I was sitting cross-legged on the floor in the meditation hall with my eyes closed. It was evening and Swamiji was giving us each energy darshan (direct transmission from the Cosmos through him), and putting us into yet another inner awakening process. I heard him take a few steps away from me, then return and touch my head again.

My mind blew open. A vision swirled into view. Tears began to pour down my face. In that gentle touch the mystery of my life's journey was solved.

Nithyananda told us earlier that he had incarnated with 2 million souls to help him move mankind to a higher consciousness. He needed people with "experience-based" bodies for his mission, because people who have lived in the world knew truth when they hear it. Monks and intellectuals that stay hidden away in libraries never completely understand the teachings, because they have no worldly experience to relate to.

I saw that before birth I had boldly agreed to incarnate in the West, and gain as many experiences as I could. That I had looked at the shopping list of rides available in this game of life, and had glibly checked off a swack of them: homeless with a baby – check. Get attacked by a cult – check. Have baby kidnapped – check. Up the creek without a paddle – check, check.

I also saw Swamiji trying to stop me from checking off even more on the list, but I brushed him aside saying "I can handle it!"

I had asked for every event that happened. Just as the Universe is continually expanding, we must expand through experience to keep up with it. Before birth I made a deal with this Avatar. He promised me that if I kept my end of the bargain and completed all these tasks, he would bring me home. And home was the core of my being - my true self that had been hiding, watching, cheering me on.

I sat on the floor and tears of relief poured out of me. There had been a reason for all that had happened. The test was simple; could I hold my centre and withstand the churning to become a spiritual warrior?

For years I wondered about the apparently misguided sign I had been given when I first met Rasta John on Venice Beach.

"This is the one you've been looking for", the Voice had said.

Why would I look for someone who would put me through Hell? Now I knew. Because of John I experienced love beyond comprehension and terror beyond belief. I had experienced the duality of Existence at its finest. And through it all our son, Esah, came into the world.

The massive churning that happened in me, as a result of marrying John, had shattered my false self, and allowed me to meet the real me.

One day Swamiji told us a story about the night fear was removed from his system. During his wandering years as a young man he was walking alone in the dark when he came upon a pack of deadly hyenas. He let out an unearthly roar and out of nowhere a saddhu (wandering monk) appeared and scared them away. But the sound that came out of him cleared his chakras of fear.

Swamiji said the event was a blessing because it permanently removed fear from his system. He said when the opportunity to experience intense fear arrives, dive in! Swim in it, experience it, let it shake you to your core. The sound that came out of him was primal, necessary, and made him fearless.

It was the same thing that happened to me the night John had me pinned to the floor, waving an axe over his head, ready to kill me and my baby. I had let out a primal noise and roared out the fear. It set me free.

That night in India, sitting on the floor crying, was one of so many mystical events I would experience around this Incarnation. Every day brought more and more exhilaration and excitement about life. Nithyananda showed me how to manifest my reality instantly, how to remain a witness to life and therefore unharmed by it. He showed me compassion and profound wisdom.

*****

While many people attending the program at the ashram scrambled for his attention, to get noticed by him, I listened to his words.

“Stop chasing this form!” he warned.

He was merely a doorway for us to walk through to reach the Divine. While people jostled for position, trying to get close to him, I moved further away. The energy that had saved me in California grew stronger. My lessons came to me in the silence. I became detached from the movie playing in front of me, and went deeper within. This is where Existence embraced me.

“You want to play an even better game?” it asked.

I did.

Every truth I learned hit me deep inside. All of the events of my life had prepared me for this. Every broken heart, every shattered dream, every frightening attack, every nut case, had created the space in me to recognize truth when I heard it. I didn't need the media or friends, or superiors to tell me what to believe and what not to. The deep knowing that is our true selves had finally become established in me, and I knew it would never leave.

While most people stay in the equivalent of a sandbox all their lives, fighting over territory and toys, I wanted more. Nithyananda told us about our soul's journey through thousands of lives and thousands of planets. But only on Earth can a soul win the game, and attain enlightenment. This is why we choose to be born here as humans, to win the game and become enlightened. And I'd found the one who could take me there.

*****

One night after we had enjoyed a cultural performance put on by local musicians and dancers, Swamiji began initiating devotees into his mission. People from around the world who had attended courses, become teachers, and had been given spiritual names by him applied to be accepted full time into his mission as ashramites. The air was charged with anticipation as the full hall waited to see who would be accepted, and who within the mission would be promoted. Swamiji explained that he was watching for each person's personal connection with God, not on how efficient they were, or how long they had been with him. He could see everyone's energy field, and through this he could see who was merging with the Divine.

I was honored to be able to witness such a sacred ceremony. Through the weeks of doing Seva, meaning 'being of service', with many of his ashramites, I had gotten to know a lot of the people in his sangha, or spiritual community. They were the sweetest group of people I had ever encountered. I cared about them as if they were my own kids.

As each one had their name called they rushed up on stage to receive a new spiritual name, and new colors to wear. I cheered and hooted with the rest of the crowd. Some young men and women had overcome immense hurdles to be with him. They were accepted one by one on a probationary status. Swamiji said it wasn't easy living around him, so it would take time to see if they were ready. He would also watch their energy over the months and years to see if their life path was as a celibate (Brahmacharya), or married with kids in the Rishi order.

I loved this about the ashram. It was like a village, embracing young and old alike, married couples, children and elders. There was a place for everyone here. Elders were respected and continued to be of use, no matter what their age. Nithyananda believed that forcing celibacy onto people whose life paths were preordained for marriage caused a lot of the 'screw loose' problems in many religions these days.

As the crowd cheered, and souls joined the mission, I thought to myself, *maybe he'll call my name.*

This idea was immediately shot down by my logical brain. I was there for the first time, and had only attended one course. I didn't even have a spiritual name. The room was full of women in saris, while I was in my Canadian street clothes. This process of admission to his lineage took years.

"But maybe he'll call my name", whispered the little voice.

Swamiji looked at me across the crowd and smiled. "Is there anyone else who would like initiation?"

My heart leaped. He'd heard me. My hand shot up in the air. Next thing I knew I was on stage, in my Canadian clothes, being initiated. He smiled and shook his head, "Do you even have a spiritual name?"

I shook my head "No". He pushed hard on my third eye and waited for one to float down from the Cosmos. Seconds ticked by.

"Nobody home?" I asked.

He grinned and shook his head. "Later", he promised.

I was given a yellow kavi (scarf) to wear, showing I was on probation, and went back to my seat. I had taken off my glasses when I went on stage, and left them on my seat. Many healers say near sightedness is caused by fear of the future, or being afraid of seeing the bigger picture. When I returned to my seat, my glasses were lying in pieces. I burst out laughing and realized I wasn't afraid of the future anymore.

*****

I was now in the inner circle of his sangha and moving through energy practices that were putting my body into warp drive. Every morning I woke up vibrating so hard I would rush to the morning workout as if my life depended on it. One hundred and eight Sun Salutations later, I would be balanced again.

I felt myself sliding in and out of different states of awareness almost hourly. I was pondering this one morning after our yoga session when out of the blue I rolled my ankle and hit the red dust hard. I looked around for the massive irregularity in the ground that had ambushed me. There wasn't one. I got up, brushed myself off, and limped off to get ready for the morning talk and meditation.

By mid morning I was in agony. The pain in my foot had become unbearable and it was swelling up in a dangerous way. I was shaking and crying uncontrollably. Apparently this is often the sign of a past life trauma being removed. Once you are under the care of an Avatar, he can remove Karma for violent death by causing a simple injury to take place instead.

The ashramites didn't waste any time. They loaded me into a cab and sent me off to the local clinic for X-rays. Now, India has an interesting traffic system. I'm guessing there is no driver's manual that must be learned in order to pass your driver's test. You just need to survive for an hour on the road and you pass.

It seems our little road to the ashram didn't merge onto the freeway in the direction my driver wanted to go. So, he simply turned onto the freeway into oncoming traffic, until he could find a break in the median and cross over.

I was in the back seat with my injured foot resting on the back of the driver's seat to reduce the swelling. The driver had a mini temple set up on his dashboard with deities galore. Indian music was blaring, and he was turned around backwards looking at me, asking how I liked India.

Giant trucks hurdled towards us, horns blaring, and I thought, *Great, I finally found an Enlightened Being and I'm going to die on a freeway outside of Bangalore!*

This insane game of chicken didn't kill us, and before I knew it, we had pulled into a small, local clinic. You would think a giraffe had just been led into the waiting room from the looks I got. I was a good foot taller than anyone there, a whole lot whiter, and they barely spoke English. I had to sit and wait for a foot doctor who spoke English to come help me.

Eventually my foot was X-rayed and I was shown the sprain, the fracture, and the mess my foot was in. As they wrapped the plaster cast on, I was told to keep it elevated for 5 days, and the cast needed to stay on for a month. A month!

I had never had a cast in my life, and I couldn't believe my adventure in India was about to be hobbled. I fought back tears as we drove back to the ashram in the dark. I hopped to my room. No, it wasn't a walking cast, and they didn't have any crutches. I had missed dinner and dejectedly threw myself on the bed and stared at the ceiling.

Many of the local women in the ashram didn't speak much English and hadn't gotten to know this foreigner who was suddenly amongst them. The cast gave everyone the perfect way to start a conversation with me. Every morning as I sat on the front balcony, foot propped up on the railing, they dutifully stopped by and practiced their English, "How the foot?"

Different ladies took turns bringing me my meals, and one of the IT guys who needed someone to transcribe talks was thrilled I was available. In addition, it gave me time to catch up on reading some of the 200 books Nithyananda had written. I was loaned a copy of *Guaranteed Solutions,* and continued my lessons in solitude.

Some of the school kids wandered by and shyly asked how I was. I taught them the Canadian tradition of drawing on casts and I soon had a dazzling display of artwork and signatures on it.

I didn't realize what a whirlwind this trip had been until I actually had time to stop and just be. I spent my days staring out across the plains at the Royal Palm trees, or studying the sacred secrets of the Vedic tradition as taught by Swamiji. I found myself sleeping, napping, and being generally spaced out.

Finally, the five days were up and I could join the other ashramites for the morning talk at the temple. I jammed my toes into my flip flops, put on my sari, and slowly made my way up the hill. Many along the way checked on my cast and made me feel part of my new spiritual family.

That morning I wrote Swamiji a note saying my foot was injured, and could he please heal it. He stood in front of me during darshan, hand on my head, and read. He must have thought I had stubbed my toe or something, because he didn't seem very concerned.

"I'll take care", he said. Then he casually looked down at me foot. Staring back at him was a massive white cast filled with artwork.

"Oh!"

He jumped back in surprise. He gave me a startled look and we both burst out laughing. In that moment time stood still. Everything went white for a moment, then I landed back in the present. He crouched down in front of me and gently laid his hand on the cast. I held my breath, then he was gone.

The next morning the cast began disintegrating and became a soft, floppy, slipper-like thing. There was no pain or swelling in my foot, and I hoped beyond hope that it really had been healed. I showed the ashram doctor and she said, “You have to go back and get a new cast. You still have 3 weeks left.”

“But he healed me!” I protested.

“We don’t want to take any chances. You have to go back to the clinic and get it x-rayed again.”

Once again I was sailing down the freeway the wrong way, while my cabbie played chicken with the trucks and buses to his loud, blaring sitar music. This time I felt detached and saw how hilarious it all was. I laughed all the way to the clinic.

The doctors didn’t think it was funny at all. They were adamant; I had to have a new cast.

“But I’m healed!” I declared and started jogging on the spot to prove it.

“Stop doing that!” they screamed back at me.

“At least check it before you put on a new cast.”

Begrudgingly they agreed and a doctor cut the cast off and began yanking my foot around, waiting for me to scream. I grinned back.

“Where’s the original X-ray?” he demanded.

The X-ray was handed over and we all peered at it. There was no fracture, no sprain, nothing. Not only had Nithyananda healed my foot, but he erased any evidence that might have kept me in a cast.

“Why would we put a cast on a perfectly good foot?” asked the confused doctor. I smiled and waved as I headed out the door.

“Whose ashram did you say you were staying at?” he called after me.

"Nithyananda!" I hollered back.

*****

Famous American mythologist and anthropologist Joseph Campbell once said we are all meant to live lives of mythical proportions. Each of us owes it to ourselves to follow our bliss.

We were never meant to stumble through life without guidance. I had searched in vain through churches in Western Society for help with life's problems. But that didn't stop me from searching. I realized there is someone out there for every one of us who will speak truth in a language we can understand. My guru may not be your guru. But there is someone out there for you! Keep looking!

As the homies of Venice Beach once quoted to me from their favorite guru, George Clinton and the P-Funk All-Stars, *"Free your Mind, your ass will follow."*

*****

It has been decades since I first set foot on Venice Beach and this spiritual journey began. As events unfolded, and the layers peeled off of me, I realized that we all live behind walls of our own creation. We create them to protect ourselves. I have learned that the one who created me, the Source that has no name, is the one we don't have to be afraid of. This is the energy that has always been there for me. The walls only kept me from seeing how amazing I was - how amazing each of us is behind the facade.

Existence can only experience itself through our adventures.

I have been rewarded every time I jumped off that cliff, every time I took a risk that everyone was sure

I wouldn't survive. I could almost feel Existence cheering me on, saying "Finally! We have a player!" Playing it safe has always created depression for me.

Everyone who has been to Nithyananda's Dhyanapeetam ashram in Bidadi has their stories; the stories of miracles, healings, and finding their bliss. The fact that this mystical being is walking the planet makes it all worthwhile. The fact that I get to be part of his "Mystery School" makes this life and its crazy adventures worthwhile.

Scientists and doctors constantly monitoring participants at his *Inner Awakening* program have found that Nithyananda activates dormant strands of DNA in people's bodies, and increases the energy production of each cell's mitochondria by 1300%. These statistics are unheard of in the conventional medical community. People with deadly and chronic diseases walk out of them with astonishing frequency.

But I don't need to hear the statistics. I always believed the world was supposed to be a mystical place, and I've been proven right. Through this Divine soul's guidance, I will win at this game. He has shown me that I am the Miracle I've been waiting for.

"Whatever happens to you, it adds to you. It makes you expand. Understand, everything in life is ultimately auspicious."

~Paramahamsa Nithyananda

(2012 Mahashivarathri speech)

WRITING THE SERB'S MEMOIRS IN THE DESERT

ABOUT THE AUTHOR

Megan was born and raised in Calgary, Alberta, Canada. She obtained her BSc in Cellular and Microbial Biology from the University of Calgary, but then spun off into a wide variety of jobs, over 50 at last count, before realizing she was a writer at heart. One of her passions is writing life histories for foster kids to help them understand their journey.

She is fundamentally nomadic and is often found hiking in the Canadian Rockies, or blissfully floating at the ashram in India.

Made in the USA
Charleston, SC
08 May 2012